Averill Nicole Richardson was born in New Zealand in 1946, where she still resides. She has an academic background in psychology and education, and graduated MA (Hons) from The University of Auckland in 1986. From a young age Averill displayed an offbeat curiosity about the meaning of life and a fascination for the topic of romantic love. These interests ultimately led to a career in relationship counselling and sex therapy. Her public reputation was enhanced when she formed a company, Couples That Work Ltd, facilitated workshops, and regularly presented her ideas as a love consultant on various national radio shows. Following her retirement from clinical practice, Averill moved south from the city of Auckland to Matamata, a rural town in the Waikato Region. There she pursues her interest in writing, both fiction and non-fiction, and is an avid follower of the performing arts. She is the author of *Improving the Odds: The remarriage gamble,* HarperCollins, Auckland, 1994, and winner of the 2019 Ashton Wylie Trust unpublished manuscript award for *The Love Path.*

To Angie and Julie.

Averill Nicole Richardson

The Love Path

AUSTIN MACAULEY PUBLISHERS™

LONDON · CAMBRIDGE · NEW YORK · SHARJAH

Copyright © Averill Nicole Richardson 2022

The right of Averill Nicole Richardson to be identified as author of this work has been asserted by the author in accordance with section 77 and 78 of the Copyright, Designs and Patents Act 1988.

All rights reserved. No part of this publication may be reproduced, stored in a retrieval system, or transmitted in any form or by any means, electronic, mechanical, photocopying, recording, or otherwise, without the prior permission of the publishers.

Any person who commits any unauthorised act in relation to this publication may be liable to criminal prosecution and civil claims for damages.

A CIP catalogue record for this title is available from the British Library.

ISBN 9781398405844 (Paperback)
ISBN 9781398414754 (ePub e-book)

www.austinmacauley.com

First Published 2022
Austin Macauley Publishers Ltd®
1 Canada Square
Canary Wharf
London
E14 5AA

My psycho-spiritual theory of love development is the product of an independent project that took place over several decades. The findings may have remained a private treasure if others had not recognised their value. There are three groups of people who have been instrumental in bringing my ideas to the attention of interested readers around the world.

The process began when I was motivated to enter a writing competition in the mind, body, and spirit genre sponsored by the Ashton Wylie Trust. The late Ashton Wylie, an Auckland businessman and philanthropist, made provision in his Will for a trust to promote love and peace within society and individual spiritual awareness. Writers in New Zealand are invited annually to submit entries in two categories, a recently published book, and an unpublished manuscript. *The Love Path* won the 2019 award for an unpublished manuscript. I am extremely grateful to the judges who were unanimous in their decision that my work deserved public recognition. Thanks also to Tim Eddington, Director of the awards, and Adonia Wylie on behalf of the Trust.

The next group I want to thank is the Board of Editors at Austin Macauley Publishers for the feedback they gave me when they offered a contract to publish in 2020. Susanna Valeriani, Holly Sheppard and Nathan Madera also deserve special mention for their warm and supportive long-distance communications despite delays due to the Covid-19 pandemic.

The third group who made the publication of this book possible is my family. Following retirement from clinical practice in 2012, I spent seven years in relative isolation thinking, dreaming, and writing *The Love Path* and its successor *The Christos and The Grail*. During this time I was fortunate that family members continued to believe in me and the value of my work. I shall be forever grateful for their expressions of unconditional love and generous material support. I therefore wish to formally acknowledge the contributions I received from Angie, Julie, Bianca, Tyler, Oscar, Imogen, Kelvin and Suzanne, Claire and Campbell, and my late sister Glenys and her husband Peter. Some feelings are too deep to be adequately expressed in words. So, I shall just say 'thank you' from the bottom of my heart.

Table of Contents

Part One	11
Creating a Theory of Love Development	
Personal Introduction	13
Chapter One	17
An Integrated Approach	
Chapter Two	22
Esoteric and Exoteric Knowledge	
Chapter Three	28
Evolution and Individual Difference	
Chapter Four	35
Myths, Legends, Folklore and Archetypes	
Chapter Five	40
Dramas of Chance and Self-Directed Productions	
Chapter Six	44
The Pyramid of Wisdom	
Chapter Seven	52
The Christos and Personality Development	
Chapter Eight	59
Love and Marriage – Future Trends	
Part Two	
The Love Path: Stages and Steps	63
A Theoretical Model of Love Development	65
Stage One	70
Kindergarten: Sensuality	
Step One	73
Infancy – Affection	
(Attachment Versus Rejection)	
Step Two	76
Early Childhood – Imagination	
(Approval Versus Disapproval)	

Step Three	80
Middle Childhood – Kindness	
(Fairness Versus Injustice)	
Stage Two	83
School: Sexuality	
Step Four	85
Late Childhood – Empathy	
(Sensitivity Versus Insensitivity)	
Step Five	88
Puberty - Idealisation	
(Esteem Versus Shame)	
Step Six	92
Later Adolescence – Identity	
(Boundaries Versus Enmeshment)	
Stage Three	96
University: Advanced Intimacy	
Step Seven	99
Early Adulthood – Commitment	
(Negotiation Versus Manipulation)	
Step Eight	103
Middle Adulthood – Loyalty	
(Respect Versus Disrespect)	
Step Nine	108
Later Adulthood – Sacrifice	
(Passion Versus Contentment)	
Stage Four	112
Transfiguration: Compassion	
Step Ten	115
Mature Adulthood – Freedom	
(Fortitude Versus Capitulation)	
Step Eleven	118
Senior Adulthood – Generosity	
(Humility Versus Pride)	
Step Twelve	121
Old Age – Integration	
(Individuation Versus Attachment)	
Select Bibliography	124

Part One

Creating a Theory of Love Development

Personal Introduction

Dear Reader,

The evolution of human love consciousness is a fascinating field of enquiry. It helps us make sense of ourselves as we are and provides possibilities about how we can grow more loving in the future. From the love poetry of ancient Egyptians; to the language used by ancient Greeks which differentiated love behaviours into eight categories; to the teachers of spiritual love who inspired religions; to the chivalric Love Courts of Medieval France and songs of the troubadours; to the popular plays of the English Elizabethan and Jacobean theatre; to the emotive imaginings of the romantic poets; to the emergence of the modern novel and on to the hip and happening social and musical movements of the twentieth and twenty-first centuries; we have evidence of the evolving ideas and behaviours that have shaped our Western cultural understandings of love. And nowadays, universal education and advances in science and technology mean information about love and sexuality is freely available.

Knowledge of love allows us to mature with positive self-esteem, wisdom and compassion. If we want our personal love narratives to be happy and if we want to live in a more loving society and ultimately a more loving world, it behoves us to examine human love development with more urgency.

My fascination with the topic of human love development arose as a result of a decision in 1984 to change careers and become a relationship couples' counsellor. In 1999, I formally announced at a counsellor's conference that I'd begun a research project to investigate the relationship between the growth of sexual intelligence and the growth of spiritual intelligence. My entry into this minefield of true knowledge, misinformation and fear-based superstition was the metaphor of a Holy Grail quest. As a result of my study, I came to the conclusion that love development, which includes human sexuality, is a subset of psycho-spiritual development and its evolution can be mapped both personally and collectively within cultural populations.

This book is a summary of my research findings.

The theory of love development I'm presenting to you is based on the notion that there are definable sequential steps of growth which can be achieved through learning when we possess motivation and self-awareness. The discipline of developmental psychology seeks to map the usual developments that occur over an average human life span and account for individual differences. However, although we have accumulated a substantial body of knowledge, the *nature and nurture variables identified thus far have been insufficient to explain huge variations in the ways adults express and prioritise loving behaviours.*

Like Carl G. Jung who argued for theories that combined science and religion, I adopted an integrated approach for my research. What I hadn't initially anticipated, though, was that I also needed to integrate the polarities of gender. A lot of religious dogma is couched in mainly masculine terms and the majority of scientific experimentation and theorising was traditionally undertaken by men. I discovered that if I wanted to fully understand the nature of love and how the ability to love develops within the human personality over a lifetime, I needed to consider feminist approaches more consciously. This was a significant step in my own psycho-spiritual development. I now believe that evolution is calling many of us to make similar leaps of comprehension so that we can better address the many urgent problems currently facing humanity and other living species that share this planet with us.

Spiritual wisdom can be found in many religions around the world, though the search requires some effort as underlying messages are frequently misinterpreted or hidden from view. To add to the complexity, Wisdom has scattered her gems wisely and seekers of truth are required to make sense of the spiritual treasures they find through the experience of their own lives.

Clues are often shrouded in parable, myth, sign, symbol and metaphor.

An integrated approach to religion alters the way we approach scientific findings. I would go a step further and argue that an expanded vision of spiritual wisdom allows us to incorporate scientific findings within a framework of purposeful evolutionary processes. Consequently, a psycho-spiritual approach to love development lets us view spiritual intelligence alongside emotional, sexual, social and cognitive intelligences. And we are free to re-interpret ancient religious teachings in the light of scientific evidence without getting caught up in any science versus religion debate. An understanding of psycho-spiritual evolutionary history makes it easy to understand why literal history has often been confused with cultural mythology and vice versa, and why religious dogma may have served an historical purpose that is no longer relevant. A psycho-spiritual approach provides possible explanations for puzzling phenomena not yet proved by science. Such as why siblings raised in the same home - including identical twins and triplets - display differences in temperament and personality from birth.

Psycho-spiritual awareness is not blind faith but rather a philosophical view of the world that allows for the existence of spiritual energy generally invisible to human sight. We can infer its existence through trial and error and the accumulation of individual life stories. In keeping with this view of reality, you can test my theory of love development for yourself and reach your own conclusions. After all, a theory is just a theory until it is proved to have validity and reliability or can be refuted by indisputable evidence.

The next point I want to make in this introduction is that all new ideas are based on ideas that have gone before. My theory is no exception. I have plaited together ideas from the philosophy, science, ancient religious texts, New Age interpretations of spiritual truth, clinical data gained from many years of practice as a professional counsellor and the evidence I unearthed during a twenty-year research project into the spiritual meaning of the Holy Grail myth. I haven't used end notes but I do name significant contributors to my ideas throughout the text and have included a select bibliography.

The nature of human love first excited my attention as a viable area of academic research when I was engaged in a master's thesis project at the University of Auckland. Beside Erich Fromm's argument that love is learned and therefore can be taught, many other theorists in the field of psychology have influenced my thinking, most notably:

Sigmund Freud, Carl G. Jung, R. D. Laing, Harry Stack Sullivan, Erik Erikson, Jean Piaget, Lawrence Kohlberg and Carl R. Rogers, Abraham H. Maslow, Eric Berne, Fritz Perls, Petruska Clarkson, William Glasser, John E. Nelson, and Donald Kalsched.

And the ideas of two Jungian therapists – John A. Sandford and Edward F. Edinger – have been highly influential in the creation of my theory of evolutionary love development.

Authors outside the field of psychology have also played their part, such as: Bishop John Shelby Spong for his argument that Christianity must change or die; Caitlin Matthews for her presentation of Sophia, the feminine face of God; Mian Ridge for her editing of some gospel texts in the Nag Hammadi collection; Tom Harpur for his explanation of the Christos principle; Richard Barber for his historical overview of the Holy Grail legend; Michael Baigent, Richard Leigh and Henry Lincoln for trail blazing a different interpretation of the Holy Grail mystery; Philip Gardiner with Gary Osborn for their rescue of spiritual wisdom contained in serpent imagery; Joseph Campbell for bringing ancient mythology alive for modern students of philosophy; Mark O'Connell and Raje Airey for their beautifully illustrated encyclopaedia of signs and symbols; Richard Tarnas for his erudite history of Western philosophical thought and Yuval Noah Harari for his intriguing interpretation of human evolution.

The creation of my love theory would not have been possible without the advent of the New Age spiritual movement which expanded into mainstream Western culture during my lifetime.

Important sources of ideas were Kahlil Gibran, Linda Goodman, Neale Donald Walsch, Deepak Chopra, Doreen Virtue, Diana Cooper, Richard Webster, Edmund Harold, Yogi Paramahansa Yogananda and Yogi Ramsuratkumar.

Unfortunately, it's impossible to acknowledge the great library of other books I've consumed over a lifetime which have also contributed to my ideas. To all these authors, in absentia, I offer my humble thanks. In addition, I would also like to express my gratitude to all the special individuals who've shared intimate relationships with me over the course of my lifetime, both personal and professional. For no discourse on love is written in an emotional vacuum.

Lastly, I want to wish you well on your own quest for knowledge and happiness. May each one of us make our own unique contribution towards building a more emotionally sophisticated society ready to solve the many problems currently facing the global human family. For when all the material goals have been stripped away, I believe life is:

A mystery to be explored.
An adventure to be experienced.
A puzzle to be de-coded.
A riddle to be solved.
And, very importantly,
A theatrical production to be played until the final curtain comes down.

With love,
Averill Nicole Richardson
2019

Chapter One
An Integrated Approach

"Mysterious love, uncertain treasure, Hast thou more of pain or pleasure!
Endless torments dwell about thee:
Yet who would live, and live without thee!"

Joseph Addison – **Rosamond**

For most of our lives love is a mystery and that is the way it should be. We wouldn't have the fun of trying to unravel love's clues if life was too easy. I therefore understand that the theory of love development I am presenting to you will only interest you as far as it relates to your own experience. This is an important point. Most psycho-spiritual information only becomes relevant when we can slot it into our subjective realities and it doesn't require unrealistic leaps of belief.

There is another point I want to make which may seem self-evident but, actually, requires some thought on your part. Most previous teachers, theorists and commentators on the subjects of love and personality development have been men. My theory of evolutionary love development incorporates many of their findings. However, the final conceptual engineering of my ideas has been fashioned by my life experience as a woman. Hopefully, this will encourage some healthy debate about modern attitudes and why they are in a state of flux.

I think it might be useful at this juncture to illustrate what I mean with reference to several well-known historical sayings on the subject of love from famous male commentators. I think it likely that many young women of today would find these observations demeaning.

- *Girls we love for what they are; Young men for what they promise to be* – Goethe (1749-1832).
- *Women still remember the first kiss after men have forgotten the last* – Remy de Gourmont (1858-1915)
- *Man's love is of man's life a thing apart, 'Tis woman's whole existence* – Byron - ***Don Juan***

Accumulating knowledge of love can be a life-long journey. Many years of academic study and twenty-three years in clinical practice specialising in couple counselling assisted my own understandings of the subject. My clients provided me with a multitude of personal narratives I found fascinating. I saw what worked and what didn't work when people attempted to make changes. On rare occasions clients made dramatic progress in relatively brief periods of time. This seemed more likely to occur when our therapeutic alliances crossed the line into the realm of transpersonal relationships. Transpersonal relationships refer to the spiritual dimensions of therapy when healing appears to take place outside conscious effort and involves a numinous sensation.

Running parallel to my work with clients was the subjective experience of my own life story which raised questions to reflect on and inevitably influenced the direction of my research. And my life experience, like those of my clients, can only be truly understood in the context of our psychohistories. So, before I outline the basic tenets of my theory in the following chapters, I will summarise some of the changes I have witnessed.

Since my birth in 1946, Western society has undergone a social and technological revolution. We've embraced new ideas and expanded our desires for thrills and entertainment. We've dreamed about life in other universes and proceeded to explore outer space. With common access to television, computers and cell phones movements for change have quickened pace. It's therefore not surprising that demands for equality in all areas of Western society have continued to be brought to public attention and children are increasingly raised to understand the rarefied concepts of animal and human rights.

During this dynamic period of attitude demolition and reconstruction, human sexuality has been taken out of the cupboard of shame, shaken down and given prominence on the public stage. This has allowed problems, such as domestic violence, rape and sexual abuse, which were formally veiled in embarrassment and fear, to surface. We are in the process of creating new avenues for justice and healing.

In New Zealand we have been encouraged to embrace and celebrate diversity. Members of the rainbow community, feminists, folk with mental and physical disabilities, representatives from our indigenous Māori community and advocates from other minority ethnicities and religions have all worked hard to find acceptance and support for their peoples in the wider community. No doubt this process of education and attitude sharing will continue. And these sorts of changes are not unique to Kiwi society as they are occurring throughout Western democratic societies.

In the field of intimate human relationships we've witnessed new approaches to marriage and family formation. In my homeland, social change has been reflected in new laws, such as: no-fault marriage dissolution; equal splits of matrimonial property at divorce; shared care of children after parental separation; financial assistance for non-working solo parents; access to abortions and the promotion of more open adoptions; decriminalisation of homosexuality and the legalisation of same sex marriage. An important step toward more openness and financial equity for women has been the recognition that matrimonial property as defined in law now includes de facto marriage. Informally, de facto marriage has lost much of its former social stigmatisation and has become commonplace, often as a forerunner to legal marriage. Fertility assistance, including donor sperm and surrogacy, have increased the options available to create families and increasing numbers of single career women are having their eggs frozen as a means of protecting their future options for motherhood.

Throughout Western society it has become acceptable, and even fashionable, to seek professional help for relationship and family problems rather than rely on the advice of family, friends or religious authorities. Books, magazines, movies, television and the internet have done much to popularise psychological jargon and demystify the therapeutic processes of counselling, psychotherapy and psychiatry.

Although we have a long way to go before gender equality is manifested in all areas of public and private life, women in greater numbers are taking responsibility for their financial futures. In the process of developing this new maturity, women are discovering that personal freedom, whether they are in committed relationships or not, is priceless and worth fighting for. The cost has been a loss of innocence and much heartache for men and women when relationships end but the gains have been formidable.

Since the ending of the Second World War, it has become obvious that personal searches for psychological understanding and emotional healing have changed the way individuals are exhibiting loving behaviours in their day-to-day lives. And as attitudes have changed, couples in committed relationships have engaged in more innovation and experimentation. Partners are now creating couple cultures quite unlike those modelled by their parents and grandparents.

The pace and complexity of modern life has produced challenges which require new approaches to household management and definitions of what it means to be a family. Many couples must negotiate the inclusion of children from former relationships. And many couples with young children do not have the practical support of older generations living close-by. Modern couples, of any sexual persuasion, generally have to learn to juggle dual careers, manage finances fairly and share household chores. Even when some time is taken by one partner to parent full-timer, most couples don't expect this to be a permanent arrangement. Much smaller families mean most of us need to consider our careers on a long-term basis and make provision for financial self-care over a lifetime.

Perhaps one of the biggest challenges facing modern couple relationships has been the raising of expectations about ongoing romance and satisfying sex. This became obvious to me in the counselling room, with increasing numbers of clients wanting professional help to establish private contracts about how sexuality is expressed in their relationships. Some couples want to explore more open scenarios, such as swinging, polyamory, bi-sexual sharing and Bondage and Discipline. While experimentation may or may not be the new normal, it does indicate that changes have been taking place in the way younger members of society are reviewing, discussing and negotiating how they want love and sexuality to be expressed.

However, despite our new open attitudes to sexuality and increasing reliance on technology – from sex toys to computers and smart phones – happiness can still be elusive for many individuals and couples. It seems an appropriate time to shift our discussion to a review of contemporary attitudes and behaviours.

We sing about love; portray love stories on screen and on stage; write fantasies about love; objectify love in design, clothing, jewellery, art and sculpture; give advice on the art of loving in therapy and in the media; and very importantly, laugh about love – particularly anything to do with sexuality – informally and in commercial entertainment. Loving gestures have permeated all areas of society. It has become acceptable to hug and kiss in public and the traditional handshake is less frequently used as a greeting though continues to be used symbolically as a sign of good intentions.

Marriage is no longer the only publicly sanctioned route to intimate happiness. The old social control mechanism of differentiating good girls from bad girls may not yet be fully dismantled, however young women themselves are changing the gender rules. And ageism is flying out the window as many elderly individuals and couples pep up their sex lives. Indeed, it's become de rigueur for all ages to play and dress-up and titillate the imagination through erotic art, literature, film, music, and dance. Partners are encouraged to teach other how they like to be pleasured and being single doesn't prevent a healthy sex life.

Alongside more liberal attitudes to sexuality there is a push for more candidness in expressing the emotional tapestries of our lives. Emotional intelligence is no longer the preserve of academic discourse and has become part of popular culture. We've come to appreciate the feel-good factor of happy relationships in all areas of living.

However, despite the progress we've made in understanding the importance of mental health and feelings of well-being for all citizens, it's obvious that within our society, and the world at large, there are many problems that need urgent attention. Consequently, conversations about love are expanding from the private lives of individuals and families to the public domains of discussion and decision making. There is a general acceptance that new approaches are needed. For the more we develop loving attitudes and skills in our private lives, the more likely we are to promote loving initiatives in our social communities and, ultimately, in the world at large.

The psycho-spiritual theory of love development I'm proposing will require further testing and review. However, I am hopeful that even in its current form it will make a positive contribution to ongoing conversations and debate whether in the privacy of personal relationships or in more public settings.

One aspect of evolutionary progress that does inspire confidence are the levels of love intelligence currently being displayed by many of our children, teenagers and young adults. It seems likely that most humans born in recent times have the potential to develop some important characteristics of love, if not all. The sort of characteristics I'm referring to are kindness, respect, tolerance, empathy, generosity, romance, passion, creativity, patience, confidence, self-awareness, positivity, tenacity, gentleness, integrity, courage, resilience, forgiveness, charity and compassion.

Learning to love better doesn't require us to join any particular religion, philosophy school, sect or political party. Most of us can progress our love development and become the lovers we want to be if we are given access to information and if we are well supported by the love of people we care about and admire.

Summary

In this chapter, I summarised some important social changes that occurred in Western culture during my lifetime. I went on to argue that this is evidence of evolutionary progress pushing us towards new levels of psycho-spiritual awareness including abilities to love better.

One way of viewing love development is to conceptualise the expected learning challenges within an individual's lifetime which promote or prevent the maturation of love intelligence. The bigger picture is to recognise common milestones of shared experience within an overall theory of human evolutionary development. I've included both these approaches in my theory of love development.

The book is divided into two sections. This first provides the conceptual building blocks of my theory, while the second outlines a hypothetical process of love development in an individual's lifetime, in identifiable sequential steps.

Chapter Two
Esoteric and Exoteric Knowledge

Psychology has always been interested in what motivates human and animal behaviour. We can think of motivation as a process because it is concerned with what initially arouses our interest, what sustains our focus and what regulates our behaviour. From a psycho-spiritual perspective, our goal is to grow our self-awareness so that our espoused motivations match our real motivations.

We can see how easy it is for motivations to become convoluted and muddled in our modern fast-paced society. We have many external stimuli and emotional commitments competing for our attention as well as our own internal needs and desires. The more complex human society becomes, the more choices we are confronted with. The issue of competing motivations often brings couples into therapy. Not just the competing motivations of two different personalities, but the internal conflicts present within each partner which maybe imperfectly understood or not easily reconciled.

Some ideas about differing levels of love development came from clients who found honest self-disclosures exceedingly difficult. Either they didn't respond well to me as a counsellor or they were so used to defending their vulnerabilities they found the counselling process not to their liking. When this happened it was a reminder to tread lightly. Our defence mechanisms are in place for a reason and always need to be respected. Modifying or removing them is frequently emotionally painful.

I'm mentioning this observation of emotional discomfort because it can apply to anyone of us. Love challenges offer us opportunities to learn more about ourselves and others if we are open to honest feedback and are prepared to articulate our emotional hurts and disappointments. The biggest hurdle for couple relationships is the manner in which such conversations take place. Unless we explore relationship problems within the safety of loving intentions and are clear about respecting couple boundaries and gender equality, we may harm couple intimacy in ways we hadn't anticipated. It's better to go softly and not be pressured into opening up too much too soon. Trust takes time to be tested. Witnessing emotional distress in the counselling room which resulted in positive changes within individuals or within couple relationships encouraged me to explore love development from a broader perspective. The modalities of counselling and psychotherapy I'd previously been trained in didn't seem to explain all that I was witnessing.

I'd been taught to query mismatches between the spoken word and body language. However, early in my practice I realised there was another murkiness which had the potential to befuddle clarity. A grey area can exist in the way partners interpret meaning from the verbal language they use. I call it a grey area because an observer is never entirely sure if misunderstandings are intentional or represent fundamental differences of comprehension. What I did conclude is that intellectual dexterity does not automatically equate to emotional sensitivity and that a lack of formal education does not preclude emotional perceptiveness.

I decided I couldn't presume that partners shared the same levels of knowledge and ability, nor that their individual motivations matched their spoken intentions. While personal psychotherapy sometimes needs to precede or work alongside couple counselling for progress to be made, it's also true that variances in physical, intellectual, sexual, emotional, social and spiritual functioning can prevent some couples ever reaching common ground. I soon learned to take notice of early clues of rigid thinking, such as a tendency to use tears as a defence mechanism to deflect the conversation away from explosive feelings or an inability to articulate relationship problems without apportioning blame to the other partner.

The healing potency of *talking therapy* is well documented. When a client retells a personal experience that is understood and respected by their clinician a powerful therapeutic alliance is formed. A similar effect can occur between partners in couple relationships, particularly during the bonding phase of falling in love. However, couple intimacy, unlike professional rapport, can be fuelled by powerful and passionate emotions which are difficult to manage well. Problems can begin in the attraction phase of falling in love, sometimes referred to as limerence, if behaviour becomes obsessive and controlling and if euphoric feelings are interlaced with excessive jealousy or a paranoid fear of rejection. While partners are usually highly motivated to make changes to please each other in the early months or years of their relationship, when sexual ecstasy and emotional exhilaration require little effort, it's easy to get a false idea about the intimacy being formed. After the hormonal flush of attraction falls away, as it inevitably does, partners may not have the desire or skills to maintain ongoing emotional intimacy. Moments of profound intimate sharing can lessen or disappear and couples settle for harmony based on daily rituals and sex. In some cases, the sexual relationship also ends or becomes unsatisfying. When couples re-ignite their sexual pleasure through sessions in therapy, they are generally also learning the loving power of non-critical focused listening, honest assertive self-disclosure, verbalised admiration and gifted forgiveness when appropriate.

Most adults have mastered communication techniques sufficiently to get them what they want at home, among friends and in the workplace. However, this doesn't necessarily translate to possessing grounded knowledge about love nor having learnt how to express genuine feelings well. And training in communication skills does not guarantee expanded emotional awareness. Indeed, the adoption of smart communication techniques can have the opposite effect if issues of power imbalance and trust formation aren't established or if unhealed emotional wounds from the past limit the physical and psychological safety of intimacy.

Attempting to deepen intimacy can be a slippery slope if lack of self-awareness or conscious dishonesty distorts the alliance being formed and when relationship boundaries are not secure. On the other side of the coin, the growth of intimacy can be hampered by the pervasive application of good manners which block and prevent experimentation, especially an exploration of our shadow natures.

As a witness to many couple relationships in crisis, I came to realise that misunderstandings frequently reflected differences in the development of various intelligences. When we are in love, it's easy to assume we're talking the same language as our partners. However, if communication breaks down, we may feel we've entered a crazy world of false accusations and misinterpretations. Of course, differences have always been present in the relationship. They are often the intriguing fascinations that spiced initial attraction, which only later turn sour when disrespect and distrust rob the relationship of its potential for happiness. Differences can also emerge is if one partner embarks on a programme of education, therapy or self-improvement and the other partner doesn't make equivalent changes.

Some clients attending couple counselling become disappointed when it becomes obvious that their partners are either unwilling, or unable, to make the changes they are requesting. When big differences in love development are exposed, there is grief around letting go unrealistic visions of domestic bliss. New awareness can help the creation of achievable dreams and inspire new beginnings or can signal the end of love stories that have run their course.

One legacy of twentieth-century social change is the search for a paradigm of committed love that will stand the test of time. Individuals no longer make assumptions about the permanency of marriage vows or promises and want to be informed about the nature of relationship they are involved in. Lasting love cannot be guaranteed just because a priest or celebrant assists in the exchange of rings and says a prayer or repeats a homily for us. We now know relationships need consistent loving attention if we want them to thrive.

With all our newfound knowledge, we've discovered love is a complex concept. By learning to self-reflect more deeply and interpret our loving experiences with more insight, we are coming to understand that love is a dynamic energy. Love offers us hope, faith, curiosity, bonding, humour, intimacy, emotional healing, physical attraction, sexual passion, affection, friendship, companionship, happiness, shared histories, creativity, encouragement, care and support. Conversely, we know that the thorns of love can leave us feeling hurt, ignored, disappointed, bored, misunderstood, disrespected, disparaged, betrayed, abused, rejected, abandoned, depressed and traumatised. We may also discover that the pain of broken or lost love can break our spirit if we let it.

While we might agree with Jesus Christ and Buddha that mastering suffering allows us to mature psycho-spiritually, we do not enter committed love relationships with the intention of learning to suffer. Suffering is the unintended by-product of life's vicissitudes and love gone wrong. So, for now, let's assume our search for love is tied to our desires for happiness. One way we can help ourselves is to become more knowledgeable about the subject of love and another way is to consciously become the best lover we can be. If we want to co-create a partnership of deep emotional intimacy and have a sexual passion that lasts, we need to become confident in our individuality and become an educated participant in the enterprise.

Knowledge is the way we describe what we know, our conscious awareness of experience and learning. It refers to both formal education and the less defined lessons of life. The opposite of knowledge is ignorance. This means any, or all, of life experience has the potential to become knowledge if we can understand, reflect on, and make use of the information at our disposal. The human ability to accumulate knowledge and use it perceptively is referred to as wisdom. The opposite of wisdom is foolishness.

Knowledge is in a constant state of evolution and is inextricably bound to incoming information, sensory experience, language acquisition, memory and reflective thought. New information is vital to evolutionary progress and our accumulation of knowledge. What is important to remember is that we are all unique individuals with differing internal realities.

Therefore, we do not necessarily process objective information in the same way.

How does it work in real life? Let's begin with a straightforward example of starting school. Most children are given a lot of information about school before they arrive for the first time at the school gate. Indeed, they may have previously attended a pre-school facility or spent a trial afternoon in a classroom. But although they may have been informed and are well prepared for school, we cannot say they have gained knowledge about being a school pupil until they become one. For some pupils, this new experience will be positive, for others it will be neutral, and for a small number of unlucky children the experience of starting school will be disappointing, unhappy or even traumatic. Although different circumstances, abilities and disabilities, will undoubtedly play a part in the outcomes, so too will individual variances in personality formation, emotional development and subjective reality.

Sex provides another example of how complex the process of gaining knowledge can be, referred to historically as carnal knowledge. We can be informed about sex in a variety of ways, and may even have secretly enjoyed masturbating, but we are still considered virgins until we've experienced penetrative sex with another person. What sort of carnal knowledge we gain will be directly related to personal experience and how this relates to the objective information we've previously received. Objective information is likely to include cultural definitions of legal and illegal behaviours, and advice about how to avoid sexually transmitted infections and unplanned pregnancy. Folk with religious parents are also likely to be receive instruction on what differentiates acceptable sexual behaviour from the sinful and profane.

The split between accepted shared objective knowledge and independent subjective knowledge may be narrow or wide depending on our age, the development of various intelligences, our material circumstances, and our unique experiences of life.

When we examine the dynamics of human intimacy, it's easy to see that subjective knowledge can be based on erroneous conjectures about what is objective truth. Intimacy may open emotional gateways but that does not guarantee the authenticity of the information shared. Relationships are easily skewed through conscious and unconscious manipulation, prejudice and deviousness. It is up to us to work our way through the mire and learn how to spot integrity in others by developing integrity in ourselves.

To help us navigate this interesting but complex theoretical landscape, we're now going to examine the difference between exoteric knowledge and esoteric knowledge. Historically, exoteric and esoteric were considered to be descriptors of opposite forms of knowledge.

Esoteric knowledge was gained by being initiated into the mystical arts. Exoteric knowledge, on the other hand, was all knowledge outside this privileged circle and was therefore considered to be factual or common knowledge. In ancient times, initiates of esoteric knowledge were chosen to join a priestly class, or were born into a cast or social group, who were responsible for maintaining society's symbolic rituals as well as sacred beliefs.

In many early civilisations, women were not excluded from religious office and could become high priestesses or virgin initiates. In later times, societies reflected and consolidated the growth of patriarchal values in religion, politics, economics, division of labour, formal education, expression of sexuality and the division of gender roles in public and the home. Esoteric knowledge, which includes feminine values and mystical intuitions, was frequently at odds with the prevailing exoteric or commonly held knowledge. In many communities, it became unsafe to be independent thinkers or hold spiritual beliefs that clashed with the dominant religious doctrines.

When it became dangerous to be different, esoteric knowledge went underground. It was kept alive through the formation of secret societies and closed sects and the use of symbolism and metaphor in literature and the arts. An example of esoteric symbolism that got transferred into common exoteric usage is the standard pack of playing cards. The four suits and numbering of the cards are based on Tarot, which originated in the temples of ancient Egypt. Tarot embodies the human quest to understand the spiritual mysteries of life, death and rebirth.

Although ancient Egyptian civilisation was in the early stages of human evolution, and their citizens embraced religion in literal terms, we can gain valuable clues about esoteric knowledge by searching for their seeds of wisdom, and others we find in ancient cultures around the world, in the light of our growing psycho-spiritual awareness.

From an evolutionary standpoint, we can see that esoteric knowledge and exoteric knowledge are not opposites, but complementary aspects of universal knowledge and what we need to do is find the clues that connect them. We can then accept that we do not need to personally comprehend all forms of specialised theoretical knowledge that can be described as abstruse, recondite, cryptic and obscure to the outsider, just as we do not need to get embroiled in the theoretical schisms of the past that separated scientific fact from the creativity of the arts or the spirituality of religion. An integrated approach to gathering clues and patterns of meaning is closer to the mark.

Like the initiates in the ancient temples of learning, students at modern universities pass through sequential stages of testing to enter their chosen disciplines. As they progress, they become familiar with the arcane language of their chosen field of study and become masters of their subjects. I believe a similar process of initiation occurs for individuals interested in developing their psycho-spiritual intelligences. My theory posits that these initiates of esoteric knowledge are groomed through a variety of life experiences so that they may be of service in the world. Many of this group are called to be leaders, teachers, protectors of freedom and justice, poets, writers, photographers, musicians, healers, spiritual mediums, designers, innovators, performers and artists of all kinds.

Exoteric knowledge is information we all have access to. Without it, we wouldn't stay grounded and cope in the material world. Esoteric knowledge, on the other hand, is more difficult to comprehend and is frequently puzzling and enigmatic. In the past, it has been scattered around the world in various religions, pockets of sacred belief and ritual, secret societies, small intellectual and artistic circles, and, occasionally, in the life narratives of highly intuitive eccentric individuals. Times are changing. Evolution is pushing us to expand our psycho-spiritual comprehension. Information is freely available in books, the internet, television, film and theatre. Whether we worship the divine formally, informally, or not at all, we can all become independent seekers of love and truth.

Summary:

In this chapter, I've discussed various ways we gain knowledge about love and how this can affect differences between our shared objective realities and our individual subjective realities. I've argued that learning to love better involves increasing self-awareness, becoming more informed about human functioning generally, practising love skills and by integrating exoteric and esoteric knowledge.

Chapter Three
Evolution and Individual Difference

We now come to the important foundation stone on which my theory of love development rests. For I think the Eastern religious belief of spiritual reincarnation is the most logical process to support a psycho-spiritual theory of human evolution on earth. While each human lifetime may be just a blink of an eye in relation to eternity and the evolution of our planet, I believe the way each of us uses our time on earth has meaning in the context of our evolving wisdom and eventual goal of self-actualisation.

Since Galileo first accurately recorded telescopic findings of outer space, and more rapidly since Darwin recorded his observations of nature during the exploratory voyage of the Beagle, our knowledge of earth and planetary history has expanded and deepened. We are compiling impressive dossiers of knowledge about many different subjects that help to explain our evolutionary history including tantalising topics like the birth of our solar system and the first life forms on earth. Although some cultural superstitions and religious beliefs have withered in the face of modern scientific enquiry, there is mounting evidence among those who possess intuitive quintessence that a spirit world does exist in an energy dimension largely beyond human perception.

My theories about love evolved over many years of research and life experience. I am now convinced that a divine intelligence exists incorporating both male and female characteristics. This divine intelligence is referred to by many names, including God. I understand this belief is personal and my approach to evolution may differ to theories held by atheists, agnostics and some religious folk. However, we can all agree that ongoing dialogue is useful when trying to narrow down what knowledge has been proved and what knowledge still awaits conclusive confirmation.

We can begin with the proven statement that evolution is a continuous process. Then, from a psycho-spiritual perspective, some of us would argue that the study of spiritual progress is as important as environmental and technological progress. If this view gains acceptance, we can speculate that integrating exoteric knowledge and esoteric knowledge will become an increasingly important task for future generations.

If we follow one of the fundamental dictums of Jesus Christ as set out in the gospels of the New Testament, our task as individuals is to search for truth or knowledge. In the Gospel of Thomas, one of the reclaimed ancient texts of the

Nag Hammadi collection not included in the New Testament, Jesus predicted that when we find truth, we will become troubled.

Becoming troubled is obviously an extremely important step in our psycho-spiritual development. I think this idea represents the rather scary proposition that we are making progress when we are not sure what is truth. And truth, or knowledge, is something we need to search for because it's difficult to find. Helping us stay hopeful that we can succeed is another promise made by Jesus, that if we persist in our seeking we will eventually be rewarded with the keys to heaven. The keys represent the clues that open doors to new understanding and heaven can be interpreted as a psycho-spiritual state of bliss.

Learning who we are and what we want to be and how to function at higher levels of psychospiritual intelligence, is facilitated by comprehending the dark, or shadow, sides of human nature and then being inspired by what's possible in terms of love, truth, peace, courage and beauty. When we understand all the choices facing us, we can consciously choose options that will facilitate self-growth as well as enrich our lives with new experiences. We grow integrity when we are true to ourselves and our highest values.

An example of what I'm referring to is the concept of slavery. We are much more likely to learn how precious freedom truly is if we've endured a personal experience of subjugation and servitude. And we are much more likely to fight for freedom for ourselves or defend the freedom of others, when we have developed principles concerned with justice and fairness.

My research into the way we develop loving values kept confronting me with dichotomies. While material evolution occurs within the natural rhythms of nature and is linked to universal laws of mathematics, chemistry, biology and physics, I couldn't be sure that psychic evolution followed the same rules. I realised I needed to link the micro to the macro and the other way around if I wanted to make connections between the observable world of matter and the spiritual realm largely outside human objective reality.

One of the early breakthroughs I had was linking the ancient religious symbol of the Ouroboros to modern scientific theory. The Ouroboros – the snake in a circle biting or swallowing its own tail – represents the never-ending repeating cycle of birth, death and rebirth or put another way, creation, destruction and recreation.

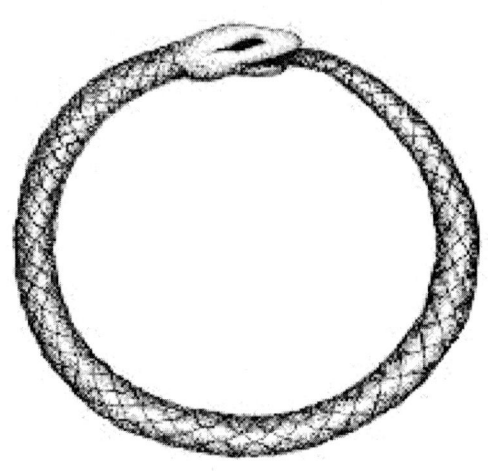

Figure 1: Ouroboros

The Ouroboros principle is as true for cosmic events as it is for human development. The Big Bang theory of creation, which argues for a beginning and eventual end of our universe, is a case in point. From a psycho-spiritual evolutionary perspective we can imagine that our universe is just a blip in a much larger story of cosmic eternity and that universes regularly begin and end. My theory of human love development is based on the notion that a divine energy was present before the big bang and will continue to exist after our universe collapses and dies. This is important in the way I conceptualise love development in humans. Love development may have begun with the basic animal instincts of mating and attachment to any offspring, but the acquisition of language and more developed brains ensured the expansion of personal consciousness and the slow growth of moral acuity. This evolutionary development, which is species specific, indicates purpose and meaning.

Purposeful evolution does not equate to all of life being pre-destined. Far from it. What it does emphasise is that human consciousness is subject to evolutionary forces beyond our current understanding. Death and decay are as important as birth and growth in all realms of material energy, here on earth and in outer space. Metamorphosis, as it is represented in the cyclical process of birth, death and rebirth, allows evolution endless creative possibilities, both materially and psycho-spiritually.

Psychic energy follows rules which can only be inferred though isolated claims of visual contact and verbal communication with various spiritual entities, and through internal intuitive processes which we come to recognise more readily as our self-awareness expands. As psychic energy is usually invisible it is often dismissed as childish superstition by those preoccupied with uncovering exoteric knowledge. Obviously, I believe this blinkered approach is a mistake.

We cannot fully explain the transformative power of numinous encounters in therapy, nor can we ignore out of hand many personal testimonies of extraordinary psychic phenomena from people we would generally classify as sane. The growing evidence of mystical encounters during near death experiences and channelled messages from dead loved ones, paint a fascinating picture of life *on the other side of the veil*. It is wise, I think, to respect what we don't know and to allow the possibility that there are reasons why spiritual knowledge remains largely out of bounds and shrouded in mystery. For it can be argued, that it would be catastrophic for us to uncover spiritual knowledge prematurely and misuse the power it would bestow on us. Better that we don't know too much, too soon.

My theory of love development rests on a belief that personal evolution is as important as collective evolution. Each of us is born with a spiritual inheritance and is in the process of evolving a soul personality or psyche. Consequently, we can say evolution is comprised of two parallel processes, material and spiritual, seen and unseen. Human psycho-spiritual evolution is accomplished through the process of reincarnation and like the material evolution of earth itself, has a beginning and an end.

I believe that over time and many incarnations, we evolve to higher levels of psycho-spiritual functioning, which I refer to as Christ-consciousness. It doesn't matter whether we use the terms enlightenment, individuation, integration, self-actualisation, God-consciousness or Christ-consciousness, the goal is ultimately the same. Through the acquisition of knowledge, the growth of self-awareness and the development of various abilities including love, we attain Christhood in our own right. Achieving full Christhood opens the door to new choices. We can leave human existence behind and move to spiritual realms beyond our current comprehension or we can choose to return to earth – perhaps for another shared lifetime with a soul mate or to aid evolutionary progress in some specific way.

Since the nineteenth century, we've learnt a lot about how human consciousness functions through psychotherapy, neuropsychology and other sciences. We can now interpret the teachings of Jesus Christ, Buddha and other spiritual teachers, through lenses of allegory, parable, fable, metaphor and symbol. Jesus's manifesto of love was clearly way ahead of its time. His message can only be truly understood in the findings of modern science and in the light of other spiritual wisdom found in different religious communities and among different cultures, around the world.

If we look back over the history of evolution on earth, we cannot help but be humbled and awed by the magnificence and beauty of nature and the growing ingenuity of humankind. This doesn't detract from Darwin's theory of natural selection and the survival of the fittest. However, a psycho-spiritual approach allows randomness and chance to exist within a framework of destiny driven evolution. And, in the end, no scientific explanation of evolution can disprove the existence of a divine energy. All that can be proved is that traditional explanations of creation are symbolic and not to be taken literally. Personally, I believe there is a natural order and spiritual justice that underpins all of life and it's up to each of us to uncover the mysteries of life on our own terms.

Science is providing us with the means to study the past in ways unheard of a mere century or two ago. We can now see patterns in the way species have developed and adapted to changing climates and specific eco systems. Some evolutionary steps, such as the development of sight in early water borne organisms, hearing in creatures that evolved to live on land and written language in early human civilisations, have been the catalysts for explosions of diversity and creativity. Yet even long periods of seemingly little change attest to evolutionary progress and contain clues about our inherent psycho-spiritual identities and our molecular connection to each other, and, ultimately, to the energy of the cosmos at large.

One aspect of human evolution that does support a psycho-spiritual approach is the psychology of individual difference. Each one of us is unique and even identical twins have independent subjective realities. We can then speculate why siblings from the same biological parents can have very different personalities and abilities. My theory is that individual personalities have unique spiritual inheritances which influence the way information and experience are processed due to unconscious learnings from previous incarnations.

A psychology of spiritual difference is given additional credence when we examine the lives of famous people throughout human history – whether they be saints, geniuses, heroic warriors, creative artists and charismatic leaders or sexually depraved monsters, fraudsters, murderers and cruel megalomaniacs. While not discounting the more predictable evolutionary development that occurs within communities and across cultures of citizens seemingly living well-adjusted and ordinary lives, the extremes of human behaviour provide evidence of differences in psycho-spiritual understanding and functioning.

Not only do we display differences in moral acuity, but we are also motivated by different yearnings. Why does one person find the geology of river formation riveting while another gets intrigued by the challenge of engineering bridges to cross rivers? Why is one person committed to achieving the peak of physical fitness for war while another wants to express their physicality through the story telling of dance? And why does one highly intelligent person choose a life of white-collar crime when another individual, from the same time and place, choose to cross the world on a compassionate mission to save peoples' lives as a doctor without borders? We could go on posing questions of personal choice for many pages. However, I'm sure the examples given illustrate the point I'm making. Scientists have discovered a great deal about how humans function in general terms, but the study of individuality is still wide open.

A theory of individual evolutionary development makes sense of suffering and justice. As we grow self-awareness, we learn to use free will for our own advancement. We may choose to be born into difficult situations or endure difficult challenges to master the next steps of our psycho-spiritual development more rapidly. I think we get a hint of this idea in the biblical saying that the last shall be first and the first shall be last. Symbolically, nothing is quite what it seems.

In support of my argument that psycho-spiritual development follows pre-determined sequential steps, I want to draw your attention to Abraham Maslow's work on the hierarchy of needs. Maslow proposed that the push for human self-actualisation cannot come into play until we have met the needs for survival, safety, belonging, and self-esteem.

Maslow's theory of human development is supported by studies in the animal kingdom. For example, wolves living in the in the wild have not developed the sorts of advanced cognitive skills that domesticated dogs can achieve. When the basic needs for food, safety and belonging have been achieved, the loving attention that bonds a dog to his human trainer can produce an animal capable of understanding complex cues. Trained dogs fulfil important professional roles in human society, such as police and rescue work, biosecurity and assisting individuals with physical disabilities. It can be argued that these special dogs have evolved cognitively and emotionally because they feel loved by their handlers and their self-esteems are raised when they are rewarded for good work.

We are only just beginning to get glimpses of the infinite possibilities of evolutionary progress. Not only will further research assist the future for animals vulnerable to climate change and habitat loss but it will also assist our abilities to manage human development in the future. For this reason, I want to mention an animal study that shows light on the development of emotional intelligence. And, as I have mentioned earlier, I believe emotional intelligence is linked to the growth of psycho-spiritual intelligence.

Dr Jane Goodall, a renowned primatologist, has spent much of her long working career studying chimpanzees in their natural habitat. At one of her many public presentations, which I attended, she finished her lecture with a brief film of a rescued chimpanzee being returned to the wild. This chimp had been badly injured and had received intense medical care and consistent loving attention from a small team of professionals before being considered well enough to cope on her own. In the film clip we witnessed a rare, unrehearsed moment, when the recuperated chimp showed an understanding of the process that had taken place. Released from her travelling cage she halted to acknowledge her special keeper by touch and then spontaneously moved over and hugged Goodall in a human-like embrace before trotting off to freedom and her new home in a conservation park.

To me, this vignette demonstrated how trust and affection can grow over time and then be expressed in body language that crosses the boundaries between species. I'm sure many of you will have your own stories of surprising responses from animals you've observed or from pets who've shared intimate times with you and your families. Love is expressed in the animal kingdom when we know what to look for and when the needs for survival and safety no longer dominate.

Several other observations Goodall has recorded are of interest to our general topic of evolution and individual differences. Not all chimpanzees parent their babies in the same way. Baby chimps who received consistent affectionate protective care from their mothers were more likely to do well in adulthood as leaders and protectors of others, whereas those who received inconsistent attention and less nurturing were more likely to display anti-social behaviour as adolescents and adults. Poorly raised chimps were more likely to be less caring of their own offspring when they became parents.

Goodall also came to the conclusion that the dark side of chimpanzee behaviour was similar to that of humans. A tribal group of chimps that had been under observation for many years splintered into two smaller factions after the death of an aged matriarch. They began to then treat each other as total strangers. Eventually the dominant group hunted down and killed the members of the smaller group; a rather sad demonstration that tribal warfare has been part of our shared genetic make-up from the beginning of time. Clearly, psycho-spiritual development in humans required the acquisition of sophisticated language systems which allowed thinking in abstract terms and higher levels of self-consciousness. We can alter our attitudes and behaviour through new learning and the flowering of various intelligences.

Goodall's research mirrors the findings of the famous Dunedin Project which looked at the generational effects of human parenting. In this study, a cohort of babies born between April 1972 and March 1973, in the city of Dunedin, New Zealand, have had their health and development monitored for over four decades. With 96% of the participants continuing to participate in the project, this study is a valuable resource for anyone interested in evolutionary processes.

The findings from the Dunedin Project demonstrate that poverty, social isolation, trauma and poor parenting predict unhappy outcomes for individuals, which can become entrenched over generations if no other positive intervention takes place. Practical situations would seem to influence the development of emotional intelligence. Taken to its logical conclusion, we can begin to improve the chances of everyone developing their psycho-spiritual intelligence by eliminating the causes of material poverty, violence and crime.

Summary:

Homo sapiens evolved into the master species on earth because they developed complex brains. They achieved this through physical dexterity, balance, spatial awareness, multifarious language, cognitive problem solving, and, very importantly, social relationships as they learned how to work together for the common good. However, despite mastering fire, maximising crop production and domesticating animals, civilisation would not have progressed without individual innovation and creativity.

In this chapter, I hypothesised that differences in intellectual, emotional, social, and sexual functioning are evidence of differences in psycho-spiritual development. When we learn to value our differences as well as our similarities, we may discover how to promote love development more rapidly among all people and then perhaps collectively create Eden on earth.

Chapter Four
Myths, Legends, Folklore and Archetypes

In this chapter we will continue to expand the proposition that human psycho-spiritual evolutionary progress includes the subset of love development. Love development can be mapped over time – both collectively and individually.

As we live in a sophisticated era of knowledge it's hard for us, perhaps impossible, to imagine the emerging thought processes of our earliest ancestors. However, we can speculate that their sensuality, spontaneity, naivety and spiritual openness resembled the profiles of our early childhoods. Anthropologists investigating some primitive indigenous communities have provided evidence that these attributes can be found in societies largely untouched by the influences of outside cultures.

While there remains many interesting topics of enquiry still to be investigated, researchers from many different academic disciplines have been able to assemble a reasonable timeline of human progress since our earliest ancestors lived in family communities, walked upright and developed languages. Current findings suggest that spiritual awareness and religious worship were universal features of early human civilisations and tended to follow predictable stages of development. Although archaeological evidence from pre-literate societies may involve some creative guesswork, we can tap into the wisdom of cultural interpreters within existing indigenous communities who have retained important aspects of their ancient inheritance. Besides archaeological evidence that art, crafts, dance and music have played a significant role in cultural adhesiveness and magical thinking, we have been able to assemble a vast literature of ancient myths, legends and folklore from around the globe.

Within all groups of Homo sapiens that manged to survive and thrive from ancient times, a process of role differentiation occurred within their social groupings. Role differentiation was not only applied to gender and age, but also to special positions of authority within the tribe, or nation of tribes. Interestingly, hierarchies of authority can also be found in other animal species where survival has been enhanced by co-operation and joint problem-solving strategies. And in the spirit world, so we are told, angels exist in hierarchies of purpose and power. Role differentiation and hierarchies of power would appear to serve a useful purpose in evolutionary progress.

With the development of language, human society was able to differentiate roles with more precision. Besides honouring their powerful leaders and great warriors, prestige could be won by possessing special talents such as designers and builders, artists and artisans, story tellers and poets, singers and dancers, actors and jesters. And from the beginning, special status was bestowed on shamans, priests, priestesses and medicine people who demonstrated they possessed a special type of knowledge. This is evidence, I believe, that psycho-spiritual intelligences were pre-existing or evolved very early in human history. Further, I would argue that although the evolution of life forms on earth may appear haphazard or random, psycho-spiritual evolutionary processes follow predictable sequential steps. While this theory cannot yet be proved, it does make sense of the efficacy of refined spiritual divination and religious prophecy.

Early humans recognised a connection to their spiritual origins. However, their need to focus on survival ensured religious beliefs had to reflect the environments they lived in. Pre-historic cave paintings and rock art from various places around the world show common themes and stylised representations. Animals could represent both food and sacred gods and female figurines, with large or numerous breasts providing the milk of life, have been found in many different places. Evidence of ancestor worship also appears to have been universal, even if the methodology employed by different cultures was not the same, for example mummification and the collection of bones versus the carving of stone and wood, and representational art versus songs and sagas.

The switch from hunting and gathering lifestyles to farming crops and domesticating animals ushered in new concepts of land ownership and organised communities. Human civilisation evolved into increasingly elaborate social groupings but remained vulnerable to natural disasters, disease, high rates of infant mortality and outsiders competing for their territory and resources. The need for strong leadership and physical prowess ensured the move from matriarchal to patriarchal dominance within most tribal hierarchies and a concomitant switch in religious worship from maternal to paternal idealisation.

When male deities became the dominant forces in religious beliefs and when societal rituals were controlled by male priests rather than facilitated by both genders, there was a loss of sensuality, spontaneity and psychic profundity. Exoteric knowledge, technical innovation, political astuteness, fiscal management, physical might and military expertise increasingly became highly valued traits within societies as emerging nations and established civilisations competed for power, territory and wealth.

Sources of esoteric knowledge became increasingly controlled and ritualised and were often treated with suspicion. In Western culture, we can see how the rise of Judeo-Christianity as formalised religion completed a hatchet job on non-conformist thinking and behaviour. It was then up to individual saints, mystics, poets, storytellers, courtesans, healers, actors, artists and groups of initiated believers, to keep the feminine aspects of wisdom alive for future generations.

The safest route for esoteric knowledge to be preserved was through metaphor, sign and symbol. That is why a study of ancient myths, legends and folklore can yield psycho-spiritual gold for the modern seeker of esoteric knowledge. While many ancient stories have been lost in the mists of time, we are lucky to have evidence of storytelling from many different cultures that have survived in written form or as oral traditions. This treasure house of adventure, courage, romance, mysticism, imagination and ingenuity stands testimony to the unperishable power of human curiosity. As a body of distilled emergent psycho-spiritual development, ancient stories belong to all of us as part of our shared human evolution.

A look at the past does not diminish, in any way, the marvellous refashioning of ancient myths, legends, and folklore contained in modern storytelling, especially those portrayed on stage and screen. From the mighty battles waged by superheroes, and epic tales of adventure such as Star Wars, Lord of the Rings and Game of Thrones, to the magic contained in places like Narnia, Neverland and Hogwarts, we are well served by those who breathe emotional intelligence into tall tales and remind us not to be intellectually trapped by the mundane mediocrity of ordinariness nor by the need for literal realism.

Any culture's mythology is a system of hereditary stories that seeks to explain the supernatural world and consequently why things happen the way they do. Social anthropologists differentiate between myths, legends and folklore based on importance and content, though together we can say these stories belong to a culture's interwoven embroidery of mythology.

Myths refer to supernatural entities who may be considered good or evil, or a combination of both, who fulfil sacred roles in relation to humankind. While they may not be real in terms of literal truth, they are keepers of symbolic wisdom. Legends, on the other hand, refer to real human heroes who perform extraordinary or supernatural deeds. Some legendary heroes become mythologised after death and their stories become embellished with superhuman feats. Nevertheless, at the heart of their story will be a kernel of truth. Fairy or folk tales appear to be fictitious entertainment, yet they too contain supernatural or coincidental elements in their stories that teach us about the complementary nature of light and dark, male and female and the consequences of wise and foolish choices.

A culture's mythology establishes rationales for social mores, customs and sacred rituals. The stories represent a human desire for identity and a sense of order in the chaos of nature and human affairs. They also represent a fundamental awareness of self, the individual in relation to others in the human community and in the wider context, the environment and the cosmos itself. When we retell stories about our origins and our place in the universe, we are expressing hope that our existence matters in some way.

Creation myths are universal, although they are not all the same. They provide us with interesting insights about our ancient ancestors as well as offering us clues to the mysteries of life currently beyond human comprehension. I will offer you two very different examples of creation myths, each with its own unique wisdom, to demonstrate common themes.

Firstly, from the Hebrew Book of Genesis, as it's retold in the St James version of the Holy Bible, in the beginning God created the heaven and the earth, and the earth was dark, void, and without form until God created light. We are then presented with a lyrical overview of evolution contained within the mystical cycle of seven. On the sixth day, or sixth stage of the cycle before the big rest, God created humans in his own image, both male and female. So, not only are we alerted to the importance of seven as a sacred number in developmental processes, but we are also given the esoteric clue that although God is frequently referred to in male terms, he/she is an androgynous energy encompassing both male and female characteristics.

The Māori myth of creation paints a different picture but nevertheless alludes to a creator god who is androgynous. The beginning is described as a void, the Nothing, or in Māori terminology Te Kore. From Te Kore came, Te Po, the night. And it was in that impenetrable darkness that the action of creation took place. Rangi, the Sky Father, lay in the arms of Papa, Earth Mother before one of their many offspring, trapped between their bodies, heard his siblings' desires for space and light, and acted. This son of Father Sky and Mother Earth, the Tane-Mahuta, who became the mighty father of forests and all living things that love light and freedom, stretched himself between his parents and forced the separation of sky from earth. According to an ancient saying of the Māori people, they were sent apart and darkness was made manifest and so was light.

The motifs of light and darkness and a parent creator god, or gods, are common features in many other creation myths. Some cultures included other interesting ideas, such as in ancient Greece when the formation of the mother earth goddess, Gaea, and the night sky god, Uranus, were preceded by Chaos rather than Nothingness.

While modern science is providing us with a more accurate picture of earth's material evolution, it hasn't yet been able to explain the origins of life in psychic terms. For this reason, mythology still has a role to play in providing us with symbolic representations of what we don't yet know or can't prove.

Legends, unlike creation myths, originate in tangible human experience. They are the means whereby communities keep alive the deeds of their greatest heroes and foster heroic qualities in future generations. Legends may also be used to ritualise group memories of overcoming trials and tribulations, such as Moses leading the Hebrew people out of Egypt and the outlaw Robin Hood and his associates stealing from the rich to provide for the poor. Legends retain an inherent truth, even though the stories become embellished, refashioned and sometimes are combined with other legends to form sagas. In some cases, heroes are mythologised to become larger than life or even ascribed divine status.

In modern democracies, we can see that the blurred lines between myths and legends are fodder for scientists seeking to discredit religions. However, if we adopt the attributes of independent seekers of truth, we can find useful seeds of wisdom without getting caught up in the science versus religion debate. The information we gather won't become personal knowledge until we can interpret it in meaningful ways through our own experience.

Myths and legends account for the past and the present, and give us clues about the future, whereas fairy and folk tales belong to the realm of imagination and take us into psychologically constructed worlds beyond boundaries of time and place. The stories teach us about good and evil, happiness and sorrow, loss and redemption, heroes and villains, magic and mystery, wisdom and foolishness, and hook into our deepest fears and aspirations. The magic of fantasy reminds us that humans have been exploring the big questions of life in hypothetical forms for a very long time, and common motifs across cultures can be referred to as archetypes.

An archetype is an original model or pattern, the perfect source of a material object or imaginative idea. The theory of a collective human unconscious with shared mythological archetypes was first postulated by Carl G. Jung. His ideas followed on from those of Sigmund Freud, as these early pioneers in the field of analytic psychotherapy attempted to make sense of recurring symbols and motifs in dreams and reveries. As is common for researchers in this field of work, their own experiences became fused with material from clients and became part of their intellectual musings.

Jung argued that repeated fundamental physical experiences of life resulted in repetitive subjective emotional reactions in humans which become embedded in their unconscious mental processes. Archetypes, according to Jung, represent our inheritance from ancestral emotional life.

Jung's theory of archetypes fits well with a belief in reincarnation. However, the notion of individual psycho-spiritual evolution alters the way we perceive unconscious processes to be inherited. For while there may be universal themes and symbols, such as the star and the mandala, it does not follow that our subjective reaction and understanding of these signs and symbols is the same. Further, I would argue, that each of us possesses unconscious wisdom retained from former lifetimes which influences our ability to recognise and make use of spiritual shorthand in our contemporary lives.

As we grow self-awareness, much that was formerly unconscious becomes conscious. According to Deepak Chopra, remembering our true essence is an important process if we wish to know ourselves and therefore to know God. Clearly, psycho-spiritual development is a very personal process that takes time. While this sort of navel gazing doesn't interest everyone, I'm suggesting that it's an essential task for anyone wishing to master love development within this lifetime.

Summary:

In this chapter, I've hypothesised that cultural mythologies carry the seeds of esoteric knowledge for future generations. Esoteric material is managed by Wisdom, the feminine aspect of the god-energy. She drops pieces of her philosopher's stone, or knowledge clues, along our paths to arouse our curiosity. These clues include the signs and symbols of spiritual language which awaken us to the archetypal knowledge that already resides in our unconscious.

Chapter Five
Dramas of Chance and
Self-Directed Productions

I am now going to move our discussion from a global perspective to a personal one. If cultural mythologies represent a way esoteric knowledge is preserved for later use, then it follows that we can map our own unique psycho-spiritual development using archetypal signs and symbols. It may begin with keeping a dream journal, creating a series of paintings, designing handcraft, taking up yoga or some other activity. No matter what prompts us to start a process of self-discovery, we can make progress in our own timing and in our own way.

Despite evidence that esoteric knowledge has played an important part in human evolution, many people in Western societies do not believe in God. They see violence committed in the name of religion and hear the rhetoric of judgemental bigotry from individuals speaking in the name of God and are intellectually and emotionally turned off. They cannot believe a God of love would sanction the suffering and misery currently besetting much of human society. And they are suitably horrified by stories of sexual abuse, accumulated material wealth, economic fraud and violent bullying that has taken place inside the high walls surrounding some churches, cults and secret organisations.

To follow the arguments I'm presenting doesn't require a belief in a specific god or religion, but most probably requires an acceptance that spiritual energy exists. A belief in spirituality supports the notion that life has meaning for all living creatures and that we are all linked to the god-energy source of love. Clearly this concept of love is beyond our limited human comprehension until we evolve to the highest levels of psycho-spiritual awareness. At that stage, we can see purpose in suffering and can also accept that acquiring Christ-consciousness requires us to address evil in all its manifestations, including the unwanted parts of our own personalities held in the webs of our own dark shadows.

My theory of love development is based on the notion that we are responsible for half of what happens to us. The other half is outside our control. A theory of partial self-responsibility helps to explain the phenomenon of individual free will operating within the communal evolutionary processes of time and place. Unless we are consciously devious, coercive or manipulative, we are not responsible for other peoples' choices, attitudes and actions. And if we innocently become victims of other peoples' hate and aggression, our only responsibility is the way we react in those circumstances.

I think this is what Jesus was suggesting when he told us to love our enemies. Love frees us from engaging in power struggles and removes the need for revenge. We can learn to emotionally detach from physically harmful and psycho-spiritually toxic situations. I admit these are not easy skills to master, but they do become easier as we ascend the higher levels of psycho-spiritual development.

One way of looking at our personal evolution is to think about our lives as a series of dramatic extracts in which we take leading roles. The best analogy I can think of is to borrow Shakespeare's contention that the world is a stage and we are all mere actors playing different parts. My argument would be that we adopt different roles in different productions according to age and circumstances and our pre-birth goals for each incarnation. As our psycho-spiritual development progresses, we take more control of our decision-making and self-talk. We learn to be less affected by the arrows of misfortune and the critical judgements of others and build within ourselves the loving resilience of hope in a better future.

When we view our lives through this Shakespearian filter, the kaleidoscope of colour that makes up our emotional worlds takes a more purposeful hue. We begin to see patterns and repeating motifs that can assist our self-reflections and ultimately our choices going forward. As we come to visualise ourselves as directors of our own productions, and not mere puppets of other people's wants, needs and ambitions, we gain confidence to set our sights high. We realise we can grow the attributes of heroes and finish our current life narrative proud of whom we've become.

As directors of our own productions, we can create personal mythologies. Not only are archetypal characters useful in this regard, so too are archetypal locations. Some examples I've used are playground, arbour, carnival, battleground, prison and temple. If you get interested in this method of self-analysis, I suggest you journal your progress. That way, when dreams in the present remind you of dreams in the past, or events in the present evoke memories of the past, you will have a framework of meaning for your own story.

If you have difficulty getting started, there some obvious ways of engaging in this sort of self-work. You can purchase a pack of traditional Tarot and use the archetypal figures represented in the major arcana as inspiration, or research authors like Carl G. Jung and his followers, or watch a lot of hero movies, or perhaps consult a therapist. If you decide therapy is the way to go, do your homework and choose wisely. Not all therapists are equal because they are all at different stages of their own self-evolutions.

During my studies in psychotherapy, an elderly tutor I admired argued that therapists cannot take their clients where they haven't metaphorically been themselves. Psycho-spiritual development is enhanced if we spend some time with someone we recognise as special because of their mature wisdom. Such an individual may be a therapist but could just as easily be someone else. It's okay to be fussy about who we consult and who we allow into our private worlds of secret thoughts and fantastic imaginings.

If you decide you like the idea of conceptualising your experience as a series of stage plays or chapters in a book, you may find the examples I've mentioned useful, or you may wish to create your own. My suggestion is to deliberately think outside the square. For example, a love arbour may represent a sexual coming of age or it may occur elsewhere in a story to symbolise the flowering of passionate romantic love. Similarly, a playground may represent the lessons of childhood, or could symbolise a period of intense sexual exploration in adulthood. By creating our own lexicon of recognisable archetypes, we minimise confusion.

Although we can productively use the discernment of others to assist our growing understanding, our aim is to create an independent intuitive resource kit. We all possess an internal wise voice as well as an external guiding angel. We may need other people to share the action of our stories in the reality of everyday life, and to provide us with inspiration and hope along the way, but ultimately, it's our own internal dialogue that determines whether we recognise esoteric knowledge when we chance upon it.

Archetypes embody both positive and negative qualities which can prove useful when we are exploring meaning in our own life dramas. Eventually, if we continue expanding our self-awareness, we can learn to view our life narratives as interested observers rather than participants chained to the wheel of life. Our goal is to have clear memories that are free of any associated negative emotion. We do not want to constantly relive the disappointment of failed dreams, or grow bitter because of perceived betrayals, or live superficially to avoid the pain of unhealed emotional wounds. A journey up the psycho-spiritual mountain is very different from a journey up the mountain of material success as they operate by different rules. However, when we have integrated our knowledge and harmonised our internal conflicts, we can enjoy the view from the summit of both mountains.

Let's return to the archetypal scene sets I listed previously. We've already touched on the attributes of a playground which include experimenting and adventuring into the unknown whether we are children or adults. Similarly, a lover's bough can represent many different things depending on age and whether we are focusing on romantic feelings or sexual passion. A carnival on the other hand is much more likely to represent adult themes. It represents a sophisticated approach to those experiences in life we can recognise as staged or arranged to impress others as well as the sheer sensual joy of participating in the good things of life.

Battleground and prison are two archetypal settings that deserve mention. Those who've participated in physical warfare or been civilian victims caught up in the chaos and brutality of war will have their own memories and emotional trauma to work through. Similarly, many personnel working with police, fire, medicine and mental health services can claim personal experiences of battlegrounds which have left legacies of negative emotional memories that need special attention.

A battleground is, of course, not always physical. It may be emotional or psychological. It may represent hurts, conflicted loyalties or guilt from the past. When we use archetypes creatively, we can see how complex one little symbolic label can become. That's why it's important to interpret experience in the light of our own special subjective understanding even when others, such as therapists, offer their well-meant contributions.

Like a battleground, a prison can represent a literal prison or refugee camp but is more commonly experienced as a psychological construct. The word that comes to mind is entrapment. A symbolic prison is all those times in our lives when we felt emotionally suffocated or physically controlled by family, friends, partners, work or material circumstances. Although these experiences feel very negative when we are in throes of depression and anxiety, they may also serve the useful purpose of forcing change.

One way of overcoming difficult experiences is to use real life heroes as guides. For example, Mahatma Gandhi and Nelson Mandela teach us that literal prison cannot quench free spirits. If we feel stuck or trapped in our situations, we can still be free spirits in our hearts. Even when we can't change the circumstances of our lives, we can choose to keep hope alive.

Finally, I want to mention the archetypal temple. A temple may represent a literal place of reverential religious worship, our physical body, or a place of intense numinous awakening. A numinous encounter is a brief spell of spiritual ecstasy outside normal human experience.

We feel touched by God.

Summary:

In this chapter I've argued for a personal understanding of esoteric symbolism if we wish to progress our psycho-spiritual intelligence. We can do this by interpreting our own psychohistories through a filter of archetypal icons. We can grow our abilities to recognise spiritual signs and metaphors by playing with the concepts.

If we wish to ensure that our fluency with esoteric language represents a concomitant growth in our Christ-consciousness, we need to stay connected to our unseen spiritual guides. It's our partnership with the Divine that ensures our reverence for mysteries still beyond our intellectual reach and prevents us falling prey to hubris. If we don't acknowledge Spirit's help and guidance, we run the risk of turning our productions into self-inflated ego trips with the potential to wittingly, or unwittingly, hurt innocent bystanders. Hitler is an example of an individual who recognised the power of esoteric symbols but had little insight about his own emotional woundedness and psychological pathology. He used his limited knowledge of the occult to boost his own image to grandiose proportions rather than embark on a personal journey of emotional healing and psycho-spiritual transformation.

The dual purposes of esoteric knowledge are clear. Besides helping us achieve personal enlightenment, we are to use our expanding self-assurance and authority to love and help others. Ultimately, we may be called in our career choices to assist the building of a fairer society, sustainable environment and a more peace-loving family of nations.

Chapter Six
The Pyramid of Wisdom

We are now ready to put the previous hypotheses together to form a coherent theoretical model of human psycho-spiritual development. And within this model, we will be able to differentiate the Love Path from other paths on offer.

My argument so far is that although evolution is purposeful, it allows opportunities for creativity and diversity. Evolution follows natural laws of material energy yet is also bound within the mysterious elements of psychic energy and spiritual justice. From the broad strokes of collective development to the minutiae of an individual soul personality unfolding like the petals of an open lotus flower, human evolution is a continuous process.

My psycho-spiritual theory of love development is based on the belief that it is possible to emulate the gods by becoming wise and fully Christ-conscious. Through the application of free will, we choose who we want to be over many, many, lifetimes. This spiral thread of eternal spiritual life, which is echoed in the natural rhythms of birth, death, and rebirth, is made meaningful when a lone pilgrim ascends the mountain of knowledge and becomes enlightened. Enlightenment is achieved through the acquisition of exoteric and esoteric knowledges which together form psycho-spiritual intelligence. Love development occurs within the larger framework of psycho-spiritual development.

Creating a model of psycho-spiritual development culminating in a pinnacle of enlightenment required me to incorporate some seemingly disparate ideas: biological inheritance; chronological age; individual differences; personality formation; theories of learning, socialisation processes, scientific evidence and relevant seeds of wisdom from religion and philosophy. I had already concluded that psycho-spiritual intelligence was complex and could not be identified by the usual psychological assessment scales that are frequently culturally and socially biased. Categories such as well-adjusted and not well-adjusted have no meaning when the articulated goal is psycho-spiritual enlightenment. Just as likely to lead to theoretical dead ends would be any religious definitions of good and evil that are rigid or narrow. During my career as a relationship counsellor my clients had showed me, without a shadow of a doubt, that even when we have similar cultural backgrounds and share the same language, the various behaviours we display represent quite different levels of love development. I presumed that which was true for love development could also be true of other aspects of psycho-spiritual development. The challenge became how to create a model of psycho-spiritual development that included all these ideas.

My starting position was the symbolic mountain of wisdom. Mountains have always held magical and sacred properties in our cultural myths as they represent pathways of communication with the gods. I realised all I needed to do was describe the ideal pathway up a mountain that could lead to enlightenment, in abstract terms. As is usual when immersed in theoretical musing, my interest in creating a hypothetical mountain inspired me to research the stories of literal mountains. This proved useful as it constantly reminded me that the task was no ordinary academic exercise. I will mention a few of the mountains to give you a taste of the vast amount of literature available on the subject. I hope it inspires you to identify your own special sacred place in the natural world.

Here in New Zealand we have many hills, mountains, lakes and rivers that are significant to our indigenous Māori people. Māori tribes [iwi] and their sub-tribes [hapu] generally have their own special sacred [tapu] areas close to their ancestral settlements. However, the importance Māori people have ascribed to mighty sacred mountains was exemplified in 1887 when the Paramount Chief Te Heuheu Tukino presented three North Island peaks to our nation. The gift was conditional on the areas around Mounts Tongariro, Ngauruhoe and Ruapehu being protected from exploitation in perpetuity.

Just across the ditch, as we Kiwis like to name the Tasman Sea that divides us from Australia, we have the largest monolith in the world, Uluru, also known as Ayres Rock. Uluru makes a dramatic statement because of its isolation. It rises from a plain to a great height and is nine kilometres in circumference. Uluru is owned and venerated for its spiritual significance by the Anangu Aboriginal people who are thought to be one of the world's oldest societies.

Moving the discussion to the northern hemisphere, I want to draw your attention to Jebel Barkal, which means holy mountain in Arabic. This relatively small mountain, situated close to a bend in the Nile River in the ancient region known as Nubia, is now part of the Northern State of Sudan. The mound was made famous in ancient times as it was believed to be the primordial creation site of the Egyptian god Amun and his consort Mut. Archaeologists have investigated the sanctuary in front of the mountain which includes the remains of temples, shrines and palaces.

Remaining in the Middle East, there is another mountain of interest to us, Mount Sinai. Mount Sinai – also known as Mount Horeb or Gabal Musa or Jebel Musa – is important in the religious heritage of Jews, Moslems and Christians. According to the account in the Book of Deuteronomy, this was the mountain where Moses received instructions for the ten commandments directly from God, through a voice in a flaming bush.

Moving our discussion to Greece, we have several examples of important ancient sites of worship. Mount Olympus was home to Zeus and a pantheon of gods and goddesses, and Delphi, which sits on the side of Mount Parnassus, above the Gulf of Corinth, was the location of a temple dedicated to the god, Apollo. The fame of Delphi was due to the presence of a high priestess, known as the oracle, who acted as a psychic medium to followers of Apollo seeking divine guidance.

Before we move to Asia, I want to mention Archangel Michael's connection to mountains and high hills. Archangel Michael is recognised by all three of the monotheist faiths, Judaism, Islam and Christianity. Archangel Michael is also important in the mythology of the Holy Grail quest. It is said that along with the Master Kuthumi, he is a co-protector of the Holy Grail. Archangel Michael's link to the Holy Grail mythology, makes Glastonbury Tor, in Somerset, England an interesting Grail site. Only the tower remains of a church once built there, but the church was originally dedicated to Saint Michael who, tradition tells us, likes to guard from high ground. A symbolic representation of Archangel Michael is again found on high ground in Normandy, France. Legend has it that in the eighth century, Archangel Michael appeared to the Christian Bishop of Avranches with instructions to build a church on a special island.

The awe inspiring Le Mont Saint-Michel is the result.

Our next destination is to be found in the Himalayan mountain range. Mount Kailash was identified as a home of the gods in the early Indian epic, the *Mahabharata.* Although we could discuss many other holy sites on the Indian sub-continent, the other example I want to highlight is Mount Arunachala. Mount Arunachala is a holy hill at Tiruvannamalai in Tamil Nadu, South India and is considered by Hindus to be a manifestation of Lord Shiva, the Lord of the Universe. Mount Arunachala is special to many of us in the West because in relatively recent times it was significant in Yogi Ramsuratkumar's journey to enlightenment.

Our next holy site is the shrine known as Borobudur sited on Bhumisan Brabadura, *The Ineffable Mountain of Accumulated Virtues,* in Java, Indonesia. This example is particularly interesting for our discussion because it has a constructed path that provides pilgrims with a purposeful climb. Originally built in the eighth and ninth century with Hindu influences, it was later altered by Buddhist adherents to emulate the stairway to enlightenment. Pilgrims and worshippers physically ascend a processional path in a clockwise direction which allows them to maintain contact with the shrine through the right hand.

The notion of a stairway to enlightenment is not restricted to Buddhism. The Jewish Patriarch Jacob, who is associated with Mount Moriah in Jerusalem, had a famous ladder dream which is recounted in the Book of Genesis. In his dream, Jacob saw a stairway that began on earth and soared to heaven. On one side of the stairway angels of God were ascending and on the other side angels of God were descending. Although there have been many different interpretations of this dream, I regard the dream as another clue that psycho-spiritual evolution is achieved through the process of reincarnation and involves identifiable sequential steps of development.

I decided to base my model of psycho-spiritual development on a pyramid shape, which I named the Pyramid of Wisdom. There are many references in Tarot and religious literature that four is a sacred numeral, so a four-sided pyramid made sense. It also was a nod to Plato who had postulated that there were four routes to the divine: poetical and musical, religious or ritual, prophetic, and amorous. Although I renamed the pathways based on modern psychological and New Age theories – the Truth Path, the Peace Path, the Warrior Path and the Love Path – I was pleased my model had such ancient origins. The sum of our progress on all four paths can be described as our psycho-spiritual intelligence quotient.

The clarification that the Love Path is one of four paths was extremely useful as it prevented me from imagining everyone had to follow the same path to reach the summit. I could see that although love development is important, so too are the developments of truthfulness, peaceful intentions, courage and inner resilience.

Unlike the path at the Borobudur shrine which symbolically leads all pilgrims to the summit of a hill, questers up a four-sided pyramid have choices and there are opportunities for different profiles of growth and knowledge. Not only can we choose a different path in different incarnations, but we can also alter the direction of our ascent at any stage of our development within a lifetime. We can ascend or descend on the same path, or zigzag and spiral according to our own needs, interests, capabilities, intentions and desires.

The basic premise of my model is that we begin life unaware of past life experience but with, as Sigmund Freud would term it, an inherent libido thrust for new life. If we use our time on earth well, we add more knowledge to our evolving psycho-spiritual development and we make progress up the pyramid. If we abuse our time on earth, we lose ground and retreat down the pyramid. The children's game of snakes and ladders represents the sort of positive progress and negative regression possible. However, unlike the board game we do not achieve enlightenment by skipping steps. There are no short cuts to Christhood.

My schema of four pathways shown in Figure 2 is based on the modern psychological notion that the ultimate state of well-being requires congruity of mind, spirit, body and heart. I have described the followers of each path in archetypal terms: [mind] Creators and Communicators; [spirit] Hierophants, Philosophers and Poets; [body] Warriors and Protectors; and [heart] Lovers and Healers.

Figure 2 also highlights the role of the angelic realm in our evolutionary progress. The four Archangels of the Divine Presence, Gabriel, Uriel, Michael and Raphael, are associated with each of the four paths: Gabriel – mind, Uriel – spirit, Michael – body and Raphael – heart. And you can take the analogy of four paths to Christhood further by linking them to the four suits of Tarot [pentacles, swords, wands, and cups] and the four elements of life [earth, air, fire and water].

Before proceeding, let's summarise what we know about the four Archangels who make up the divine presence. While all Archangels are interested in assisting all of humanity and can be called on by individuals seeking help or guidance, the four Archangels of the divine presence have been assigned responsibility for specific areas of intelligence and psychospiritual growth.

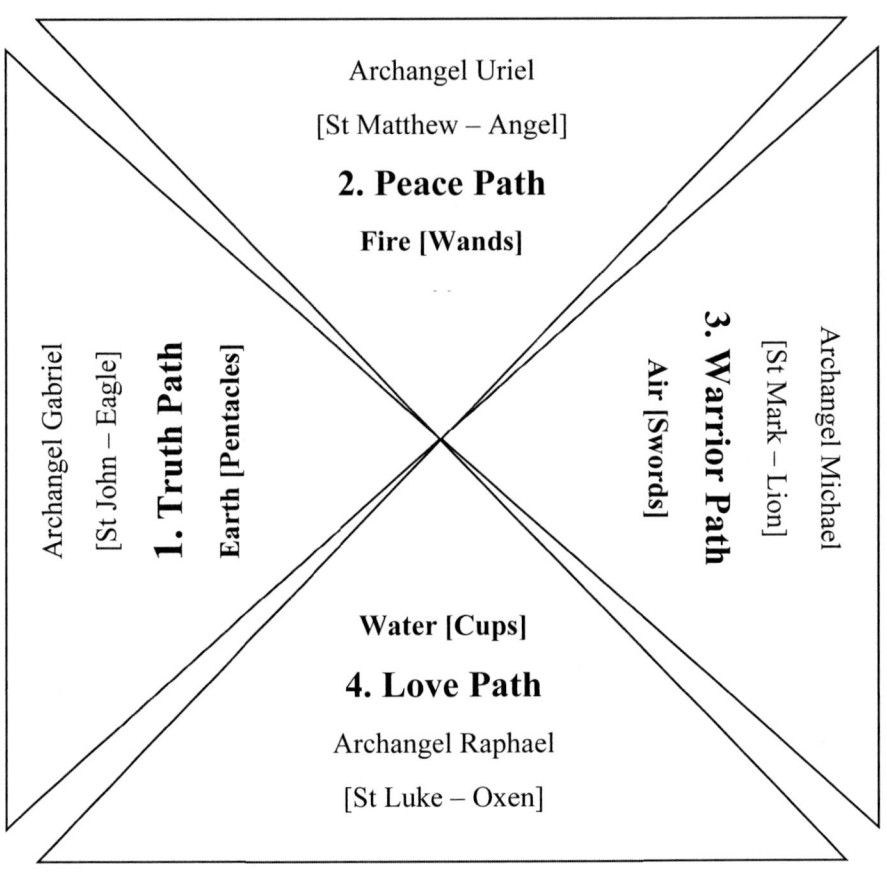

Figure 2: The Pyramid of Wisdom, comprised of four paths – Truth, Peace, Warrior and Love.

[Designed by Imogen Bunting]

Archangel Gabriel oversees communication and creativity and is the patron saint of writers, journalists, photographers, creative thinkers, actors, producers and performers of all kinds. He is available to guide those in business, justice, politics and farming. He assists inspirational creativity across many fields of human endeavour including architecture and engineering, film making, fine dining, fashion, garden design, jewellery and aesthetic delight. Gabriel is also well known as the angel of childbirth and was the messenger who prepared Mary for the arrival of her special son, Jesus.

Archangel Uriel oversees human activity concerned with peace and salvation. He was the angel responsible for providing humankind with the Kabbalah and the heavenly mysteries of the Arcana which the alchemists sought to unravel in the Middle Ages. He assists writers of esoteric and exoteric knowledge, including poetry, music, mathematics, philosophy, science, history and science-fiction fantasy. He can provide guidance for religious devotees and hierophants, teachers of higher learning, artists and artisans including technical designers of watches and musical instruments. He is the patron saint of all who work for peace and diplomacy.

Archangel Michael represents the image of the Christ-conscious warrior, or the legendary perfect knight of the Holy Grail saga, prepared to fight the dark forces in the service of goodness and light. He assists individuals concerned with developing resilience and personal integrity. He is the patron saint of those serving in the armed forces, police, firefighting and ambulance services. He is a guide for all those concerned with physical discipline and maximising personal potential, such as sport, dance, martial arts, acrobatics, travel and labouring in many fields such as farming, fishing, forestry, housing, environmental projects, road making and construction. He is available to help anyone seeking courage in leadership roles and for those actively defending love, truth, justice, and freedom.

Archangel Raphael oversees all who are promoting love and healing in the world through their career choices or caring roles in the home and community. He is the patron saint of doctors and nurses, veterinarians, animal rescuers and protectors, teachers of the young, social workers, psychotherapists and counsellors. He provides guidance for all those seeking to heal the planet in practical ways including environmental science, art and design, recycling of material waste, singing and song composition, food and beverage preparation, charitable enterprises and philanthropic projects, and charismatic leadership roles. As we prepare for a new epoch in human evolution, he is particularly concerned with assisting individuals who wish to develop more loving characteristics within themselves.

Each path up the Pyramid of Wisdom is comprised of twelve steps. The steps of development may differ in specifics between paths but are thematically aligned to one another. The twelve steps are divided into four major stages. Each stage is therefore comprised of three steps linked to each other by maturational imperatives. Although language and tasks may differ between paths, the steps on all paths progress to the summit. We can follow any path of choice and move sideways from one path to another, but we are prevented from ascending to the immediate step above us until we have mastered the required challenges of development on our current step. It is theoretically possible that the Love Path is the most difficult route to master.

The pyramid shape of the model reminds us that the ancient Egyptians built their literal pyramids because of their religious beliefs. They were designed not only as visible manifestations of each Pharaoh's power in life and death, but to physically assist the dead Pharaoh's route through the underworld to their rightful place in the heavens with the gods.

Because the deceased Pharaoh's ka (spirit) needed to be reborn in the new Pharaoh, the Ancient Egyptians had some complicated beliefs about the role of the body in the process of reincarnation. Consequently, pyramids were consecrated burial sites with mystical meanings which don't translate well into modern understandings. However, within their religious mythology we can still find seeds of wisdom in symbolic form if we search carefully.

Besides Jacob's ladder dream, there is another reference in Judeo-Christian literature that supports the idea of spiritual reincarnation. The myth about the Tower of Babel, as recounted in the Book of Genesis 11: 1–19, warns us about the dangers of ascending the stairway of knowledge too quickly. Some modern scholars have attempted to link this biblical story to the ancient Babylonian ziggurat, Etemenanki, which was built to symbolise the foundation of heaven and earth and was dedicated to the Mesopotamian god Marduk. While the Hebrew tale may contain Babylonian influences, I think the underlying message of the story is a warning about hubris. We may possess a lot of information about a lot of topics, but unless we've done the important work of transforming our own natures, we will be prevented from completing the ascent of the tower of knowledge.

In the Genesis version of the Tower of Babel story, the construction of the tower is halted before completion because the builders can no longer communicate with one another. God has issued them all with different languages which confounds the project and scatters the workers to various other places on earth. I interpret this to mean that the builders of the tower weren't ready, in evolutionary terms, to link together exoteric and esoteric knowledges. In other renditions of the tower myth found in other cultures, the tower itself may be destroyed or the people are unwittingly thrown out. In all examples, the underlying message is the same. The acquisition of wisdom is a long and complex process and includes the growth of true humility and purity of thought and intention.

At some stage of our personal evolution we become curious about the mysteries of life and begin a series of incarnations with more self-awareness and more openness about engaging in conversations about what constitutes objective knowledge and what constitutes faith in a spiritual existence beyond our earthly understanding. This level of development is characterised by increased determination to reach self-chosen goals, the necessary discipline to achieve results and more concern for the welfare of others. Eventually, over many incarnations, we are *called* to use our blossoming expertise in the service of Spirit even if we fail to recognise our career path in these terms. When we attain enlightenment, we may choose to be freed from the human cycle of existence or we can decide to return for further purposeful missions on earth.

Questers of knowledge who reach the upper levels of the Pyramid of Wisdom for the first time must pass some initiation tests that are exceedingly challenging and emotionally difficult. However, if we stay the course and reach the summit, we are awarded mantles of psychic gold to celebrate our completed journeys to Christhood. These mantles protect us from any future psychic attack by those who wish us ill. We can still be hurt physically or emotionally, or even murdered. However, our soul personalities are now permanently protected and cannot be maimed or destroyed. We can now be described as *'one of the immortals'*.

Summary:

In this chapter, I presented my theoretical model of psycho-spiritual development, the Pyramid of Wisdom. This is an important backgrounder to my model of love development which is described in more detail in Part Two. An expanded view of spiritual reincarnation underpins the importance of free will. It is up to us whether we embark on a quest for wisdom, or not. The only requirements are honest intentions and a desire to leave this world a better place for having been here.

Chapter Seven
The Christos and Personality Development

In this chapter we will integrate the Eastern religious idea of reincarnation with the ancient religious concept of the universal Christos and marry these strands of belief to modern Western psychological theories of personality development.

Let's start with the hypothesis that we begin life on earth with a pre-existing soul personality formed in earlier experience. The exception would be newly formed soul personalities, although this seems unlikely for humans on earth in the twenty-first century. Most important is the idea that our pre-existing soul personality influences the development of our uniqueness in this lifetime alongside biological inheritance, social conditioning, opportunities for new learning and the exercise of free will. Recent interest in exploring psycho-spiritual approaches to heal neuroses and more pronounced mental illnesses such as suicidal idealisation, is evidence that many in the healing professions are expanding their thinking. Integrating Eastern and Western philosophies with science and technology is altering our perceptions about what constitutes personality formation and how it evolves during an individual lifetime.

My theory of love developmental is based on the hypothesis that each person accumulates knowledge over many lifetimes and, in the process of doing so, experiences many different life narratives. Personality formation within a lifetime is more than a product of nature and nurture, as it is profoundly influenced by the individual's unique psycho-spiritual inheritance or soul personality.

We begin life with a soul personality that can assist our goal to reach self-actualisation. As we grow Christ-consciousness, we are more likely to make choices that align with our highest truths. This does not discount the hard work our human personalities put in to be successful in the objective world of earthly endeavour. However, priorities alter as we progress up the Pyramid of Wisdom and the goal of personal integrity becomes increasingly valued. If we evolve our psycho-spiritual intelligence to a level we haven't reached in previous lifetimes, our soul personality is positively enhanced through the efforts of our current personality. Conversely, if we ignore our own wisdom and consciously choose to be less than who were before, our soul personality suffers a setback.

The process of reincarnation allows for karmic justice to underpin some human motivations and for soul mate or soul personality recognition to occur. It also helps to explain why we may choose particularly difficult life paths at various stages of our personal evolutions and why an individual with special talents may have a sense of events unfolding in a serendipitous fashion. Although theories of self-chosen destinies can't yet be proved or disproved, we can begin to gather evidence of individual experiences in a more systematic fashion.

Like Tom Harpur, I believe we are all born with a spark of god energy, called the Christos. In this way we can all claim to be sons and daughters of a mother-father god energy. Through experience and the exercise of free will, we can choose to become more Christ-conscious if we wish to. Increasing Christ-consciousness does not alter the true essence of our soul personality but adds complexity to our personality development within the current life span. This complexity is then incorporated into our soul personality when we die or when we achieve enlightenment.

If we choose to commit suicide as the method of exiting life because of unbearable physical, mental or emotional pain, we do not automatically extinguish our soul personalities. As I understand it, folk who suicide generally choose to continue the cycle of reincarnation, after some healing and mentoring on the other side. The exception is the rare case of destiny driven suicide for love of others. In this instance, making a conscious sacrifice might exempt the individual from needing to continue the human cycle of evolution. To suicide because of spiritual torment and thereby give up all claims of immortality is a different matter and is a topic beyond my current understanding. However, I accept in theory that not all soul personalities are immortal. In the *Apocalypse of Peter*, part of the Nag Hammadi collection of texts, Jesus made the statement that *not every soul is of truth and of immortality*. There is also a reference in that gospel to the '*race of immortal souls*'. I imagine the choice to be mortal or immortal is the ultimate outcome of free will.

While my ideas about personality formation have been heavily influenced by pioneers in this field of psychological research – notably Sigmund Freud, Carl C. Jung and Eric Berne – I wanted to construct a theoretical model of development that demonstrated the link between the persona of current life personality and the inherited soul personality.

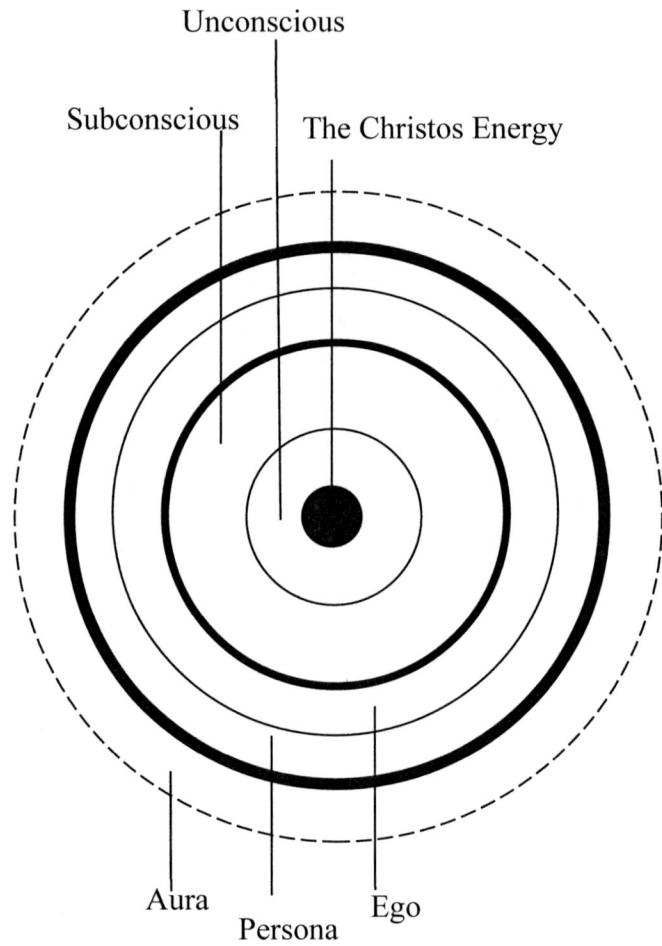

Figure 3: The Christos and Personality Development.

Figure 3 represents the summary of my ideas. The Christos is the central starting position of personality development; our connection to the universal source of love and life. This universal psychic energy field is often referred to as The Ground of All Being. The Christos energy feeds the unconscious which contains our soul personality, in Jungian terminology referred to as Self.

The unconscious holds past life material and any memories from this life lost to us because of their immaturity, because of injury or disease, or because of conscious repression. The unconscious communicates its wisdom largely through dreams and intuition and through the esoteric language of feelings, signs, symbols and metaphors. Unfortunately, if the vulnerable psychic membranes holding this material are breached through war, violence, sexual abuse and other kinds of trauma, including the misuse of hallucinatory drugs, the individual may not be able to control the stem of information into consciousness which includes both light and shadow. This can result in catastrophic outcomes for mental health and interpersonal behaviour.

The subconscious holds all memories readily available to us when appropriate cues bring them into conscious memory. The subconscious acts as a go-between the unconscious soul personality and the conscious personality. Besides being a conductor of information, the subconscious functions as an enormous storage system. It contains all collected information, both experiential and non-experiential in increasingly sophisticated and intricate units of meaning. As we age, we often have problem with cues of retrieval losing their fitness. And sometimes circumstances, such as trauma and disease, result in damage beyond repair and information is lost to the unconscious. Dysfunctional cues can sometimes be repaired or replaced in children and young adults with time and conscious effort. The spontaneous appearance of seemingly forgotten material, such as clear childhood memories in our advanced years, is evidence that cue formation and maintenance is a life-long cognitive activity in a healthy brain. The subconscious prevents the conscious parts of our personality being swamped with too much information at any one time. We understand the benefits of this aspect of our personality structure when we take time to problem solve, obvious examples being chess, work, study and counselling.

The conscious part of our personality contains the ego which is encapsulated within the socially created persona. The ego, which is also known as the true ego in some psychological literature, has access to material stored in the subconscious, the accumulated wisdom of the unconscious and information at hand from the persona. Incoming information is filtered through the coping strategies and defence systems of the persona.

The ego begins life with an uncomplicated access pathway to the Christos energy and the unconscious material of our soul inheritance. However, as we are socialised into our family and community cultures and our energy focus is dominated by the needs to survive, thrive and belong, the pathway to our spiritual consciousness tends to become forgotten or neglected. Unless we address this challenge consciously at various times during our development, access to the pathway may become permanently blocked. The old adage, use it or lose it, is apposite for this process. Self-awareness is vital for psycho-spiritual development. The Christos pathway clears and strengthens whenever we consciously embark on a programme that assists self-actualisation. Practice yields results. We gain better access to the unconscious as we learn to interpret the esoteric language of our spiritual inheritance. The ego is responsible for our conscious will and is therefore the principal driver of conscience. Its task is to maintain homeostasis between competing internal and external needs and motivations and to promote feelings of wellbeing.

The persona is the new personality created so that we can survive and thrive in the material world in our current incarnation. The persona in literature is often referred to as the false ego because its origins reside in the material reality of everyday life. This can be misleading because the role of the persona is crucial in our development and protects us in necessary ways. We need a healthy persona if we are to develop a workable conscience and avoid the worst effects of mental illness. Although important in our overall development, the persona gradually loses its dominance in our decision making as we become more self-aware and our psycho-spiritual intelligence evolves.

Emanating from our total being is a psychic energy soul print referred to as aura. Some folk, with the highly developed spiritual gift of clairvoyance, claim they can differentiate an individual's current state of mood and general health through the colour of their aura.

As we mature physically, we are offered opportunities for psycho-spiritual growth. This can alter the profile of our personality so that the various components alter their size and composition. For example, the unconscious diminishes in size if we receive information about past-life experience in order that we learn not to repeat past mistakes. However, if past life material is inaccurate or merely interpreted as former glory it can inflate our egos unnecessarily and inhibit honest self-reflection.

Edward F. Edinger postulates that the process of moving between an inflated and a deflated ego is probably common throughout our lives. I would argue that individual differences in psycho-spiritual intelligence make this generalisation difficult to accurately assess. Of course it's all in the semantics we use, whether we are we referring to the persona, the ego or the soul personality. A highly evolved soul personality may contribute to an individual appearing to have an inflated ego because they are extremely confident and sure of their own worth. Undoubtedly, an inflated ego is an essential part of the process of experiencing oneself as a unique individual, especially during our formative years. It assists the growth of confidence and promotes motivation. In common terminology, it gives us swagger. A deflated ego is a natural consequence of objective reality challenging subjective reality. A deflated ego can lead to anxiety and depression, or it can quick start a search for healing and understanding. When we accept that life's lessons are a normal feature of biting the apple of experience, we can learn to take disappointments and the critical judgements of others in our stride.

We are all vulnerable to emotional wounding. Emotional wounding can be the result of trauma and abuse but can also occur in more ordinary situations of feeling ignored, criticised, rejected, abandoned, put down, ridiculed, unfairly punished, demeaned or misunderstood. As we advance up the Pyramid of Wisdom and expand our self-awareness, we learn how to master the hard lessons of life. However, just occasionally an ego deflation is caused by the removal of a mystical veil of illusion which is beyond our control. This always causes emotional angst. An example would be the loss of a much-loved partner unexpectedly deciding to leave a marriage relationship of many years for a new lover.

The health of our ego is vital if we wish to ascend the Pyramid of Wisdom. The ego is the representative voice of our soul personality in this lifetime and provides a direct link to intuition and our core Christos energy. If the ego is attacked too ferociously by external forces, or loses access to unconscious wisdom, the persona becomes the major decision-making mechanism.

If the ego comes to rely on the information provided by the persona at the expense of intuitive wisdom, our overall consciousness becomes vulnerable to self-grandiosity. We are likely to misunderstand or ignore important universal spiritual boundaries, resulting in error and sin. Deceit breeds deceit, as truth becomes too emotionally painful to bear. The individual uses their defence mechanisms to create an acceptable reality of themselves which prevents psycho-spiritual growth. As the connection to the Christos weakens or dies completely, the ego increasingly relies on distorted information from the socially constructed persona.

The persona's size is not fixed but fluctuates according influences and pressures from the prevailing social milieu. It's important we develop a robust persona in our early development. It acts as a bulwark to prevent mental illness and ultimately assists in the prevention of acting out suicide ideation. Factors affecting the development of a healthy persona are: feeling loved; being supported materially including the necessities for physical growth, education and survival; feeling affirmed in our abilities when we try our best; believing we are acceptable as an individual the way we are; having a sense of belonging to a community; and possessing a conceptual framework on which to build a sense of trust in life and values to live by.

When we choose to complete the final stage of psycho-spiritual development, we will undergo a process that integrates the persona and ego. But more of that in Part Two. For now, let's discuss the role of Spirit in our personality development and psycho-spiritual evolution. For my theory rests on the belief that human evolution is purposeful and each of us is important in the totality of the cosmos and eternity.

One piece of religious belief I found particularly helpful for my theory was the existence of the fallen angels. Early in my research I had pondered on the purpose of the dark divine power known by many names including Lucifer, the Devil and Satan. Like Judas Iscariot in the New Testament gospels, I queried if devils existed, and if so, what was their true purpose. When I decided to view everything from a symbolic perspective, pieces of the puzzle fell into place, including the role of the fallen angels. I could see that if love and knowledge are the evolutionary goals of humanity, spiritual adversaries are a necessary part of our experience. The process of enlightenment requires us to integrate light and dark and lose all fear of the supernatural. In religious terms, it requires us to cease being afraid of God and Satan and learn to love them both for the roles they play in our developing understanding.

Some religious scholars have estimated that a tenth of all angels became fallen angels and in their fallen state retained their rank. Lee Faber has listed their names and, even if some have mistakenly been omitted or duplicated in some way, the number is impressive as is the clue that these angels have retained their ranks. My conclusion is that the fallen angels have volunteered, or have been specially chosen, to act as spiritual adversaries for the duration of human evolution on earth. My hunch to consider Lucifer and the other fallen angels in a positive light was later confirmed for me when I came across Richard Webster's account of a pre-Christian tradition in ancient Eastern writings that Lucifer has been sent on a special assignment by God to test humankind.

It makes sense that Lucifer and the hierarchy of fallen angels are responsible for ensuring we encounter the shadow sides of our natures. They have been given the freedom to seduce, teach, tempt, corrupt, gossip, manipulate, lie, falsify, harass and attack. They have the powers to entice willing and psycho-spiritually immature individuals to form into groups or armies that behave in cowardly and evil ways. Their main purpose is to test each human soul on its journey to self-actualisation. However, in the wider process of collective human evolution, they play a useful and active role in community, national and international affairs.

Truly, I do believe that life is a testing ground and we are being encouraged to grow up spiritually. By learning to know and love ourselves, we come to know and love God. Evolution is pushing us toward change. My prediction is that increasing numbers of people will complete their journeys to Christhood in the coming generations. And, given the Biblical promise that angels will be sent to weed and harvest the crop during the last days of the current age, we will gather more and more evidence of angelic assistance in human affairs including the fascinating process of personality development.

Summary:

In this chapter I've argued that the Christos is a universal inheritance which provides each of us with a spark of god energy to create our own unique and exciting personalities. The Christos is our link to the Ground of All Being and ensures we remain connected to the wider cosmos. Christ-consciousness prevents hubris running amuck and turning us into supernatural monsters. According to the theory I've outlined, the purpose of individuality is not only to actualise our potentials in the world but to internally master suffering. It is through the evolution of our soul personalities that we achieve the goal of Christhood. We can then choose a love-filled immortal existence consciously connected to all living things.

Chapter Eight
Love and Marriage – Future Trends

In this final chapter of part one, I'm presenting some ideas on future trends in love and marriage which may be right on the mark or far from it. Your role is to think about the topics raised and form some opinions of your own which will help promote or prevent such change occurring.

- While marriage for life may continue to be our cultural mythologised ideal of romantic happiness, it will not be the reality for many people. A more likely paradigm to emerge will be marriage for love. Then couples will only remain together if both partners are happy with their relationship or if both partners believe future happiness is possible and is worth striving for.
- Attitudes and values about sexuality within committed relationships will continue to change and evolve. As limiting family size is likely to become an international imperative, managing fertility will become increasingly important. And because we now understand that liberated women have similar sex drives to men, heterosexual couples will need to consider how to ensure both partners are happy with their sexual relationship.
- Singles living independently, will have increasing freedom to maintain lifestyles that support exciting romance and pleasurable sex whether or not they are in committed partnerships. Some singles may choose to embrace celibacy for intermittent periods for self-growth or permanently if they are undertaking religious vocations on the Peace Path.
- Gender equality will continue to progress over the coming decades. This will affect the way girls are raised. Girls will be taught to take responsibility for their personal finances, career paths, partner choices and ongoing sexual happiness.
- Gender equality will also dramatically alter the way boys are raised. They will be taught that becoming emotionally intelligent is sexually attractive and that there are skills they can learn to help the development of intimacy in long-term love partnerships.
- Gender equality will continue to change the way couples in heterosexual marriage relationships negotiate roles and responsibilities. When partners are joint income earners, there is more flexibility about how

- time is spent together and away from the home. Co-parenting will be viewed as a lifelong commitment whether or not the marriage lasts.
- The process of couple attraction and commitment will continue to evolve as love skills are developed to greater levels of competency among greater numbers in the community. More emphasis will be given to admiration, sexual chemistry, shared values and shared humour when choosing partners for short or long-term commitments and less emphasis on income, material assets, social status and parental approval.
- As we grow self-awareness and become more confident about expressing our intimate needs and desires directly without playing mind games or resorting to manipulation, we will be able to discuss what we really want in terms of romance, eroticism and sexual fantasy. This will provide an opportunity for partners with past hurts, such as disloyalty and trauma, such as childhood sexual abuse, to be honest about their vulnerabilities and insist that trust comes before experimentation.
- Many people of all sexual persuasions will spend greater periods of their lives as singles. This will enhance love development as aloneness, if used well, provides the ideal teaching ground for expanded self-awareness.
- Environmental degradation and climate change will force us to face the global problem of overpopulation. As a direct consequence, more people will choose to be childless. I predict private contracts will become popular which will allow childless individuals and couples opportunities to bond with specific families in return for undertakings of time and financial support. This way, all children born in the future will have better access to health service, education and a variety of other experiences.
- When marriage is conditional on both partners being happy, we are likely to see some improvements in behaviour. Individuals will develop the art of loving assertiveness and couples will be motivated to master the different skills needed for teamwork, debate, and seduction.
- Pre-nuptial legal contracts will become commonplace, particularly for relationships that begin with a wide discrepancy of assets and income or when either or both partners have children from previous relationships.
- Informal pre-nuptial agreements, whether verbal or recorded, will also become more popular. These expressions of intent can be revised at any time and will cover topics such as sexual boundaries, drug taking, respectful communication, in-laws, ex-partners, stepchildren and maintaining violence-free home environments. Some folk might want to include an annual review of relationship satisfaction.
- Parents who take time out of their careers to raise children will be financially compensated, either by the state or by the way assets are divided in the case of later separation or divorce.
- When we stop trying to possess one another and accept that happy marriages are only possible if both partners are happy, we will support

- universal couple counselling and personal psychotherapy for those who want it.
- Given the contention that the God energy is androgynous, both male and female, it seems logical that evolution is leading human development toward an integration of our gender polarities. This view makes sense of the mushrooming rainbow community around the globe. It also explains the push for many who classify themselves as heterosexual to explore the opposite characteristics of their explicit gender identification in appearance, careers, family roles, sports and other activities.
- In enlightened communities, the sex industry will be given a complete overhaul. Sexual abuse and sex slavery will not be tolerated and the rights of minors to be free of exploitation will be sacrosanct. Careers in the sex industry for consenting adults will have more social acceptance and pleasure establishments will be better monitored for health and safety.
- Not everyone will have the courage and self-belief to follow love's call. Fear of poverty or fear of family and societal disapproval will dictate many peoples' behaviour for some time to come. It therefore behoves those of us who do give priority to love in the way we live to do so in style. *Let our little lights shine.*

Summary:

In this chapter, I've presented some ideas for future discussions. Whether marriage is de facto or legal it is a human institution that will continue. And despite modern marriage being vulnerable to break down, it doesn't follow that we should eliminate the risk. Every relationship we engage in has the potential to teach us about love. We are lucky if we have one special marriage partner until we die. However, there is no requirement to ever be married if we wish to become a master of love. It's perfectly possible to become a master of love knowing only one lover and perfectly possible to become a master of love knowing many lovers. There is no right or wrong way, just many ways to find love and, ultimately, to fulfil our own potentials.

Part Two

The Love Path:
Stages and Steps

A Theoretical Model of Love Development

The Love Path is one of four paths that comprise the Pyramid of Wisdom. All four paths require individuals to master psycho-spiritual stages of development in sequential order. While the focus of the tasks may differ between the paths, the goal of self-actualisation is the same for all paths.

The model of love development shown in Figure 4 demonstrates how the capacity to love can deepen and broaden over a human life span. The chronological template is a guide only. Individual potential is affected by biological and spiritual inheritances, cultural mores, education, physical living conditions and personal experience. Without further research we cannot say whether the age and stage format presented in my theoretical model is typical or atypical. I suspect it will probably need adjusting in the future as more individuals expand their psycho-spiritual intelligences at earlier ages.

The ideas contained in this theory of love development are a mixture of philosophy, religion and science. However, my work has been heavily influenced by the teachings of two historical manifestations of love development, Jesus Christ and Buddha. Like John A. Sanford, I believe Jesus was special because he taught that the journey to self-actualisation, which he described as finding the keys to heaven, was an internal unfolding of the whole personality within the individual. He recognised this development was deeply personal and dependent on individual free will.

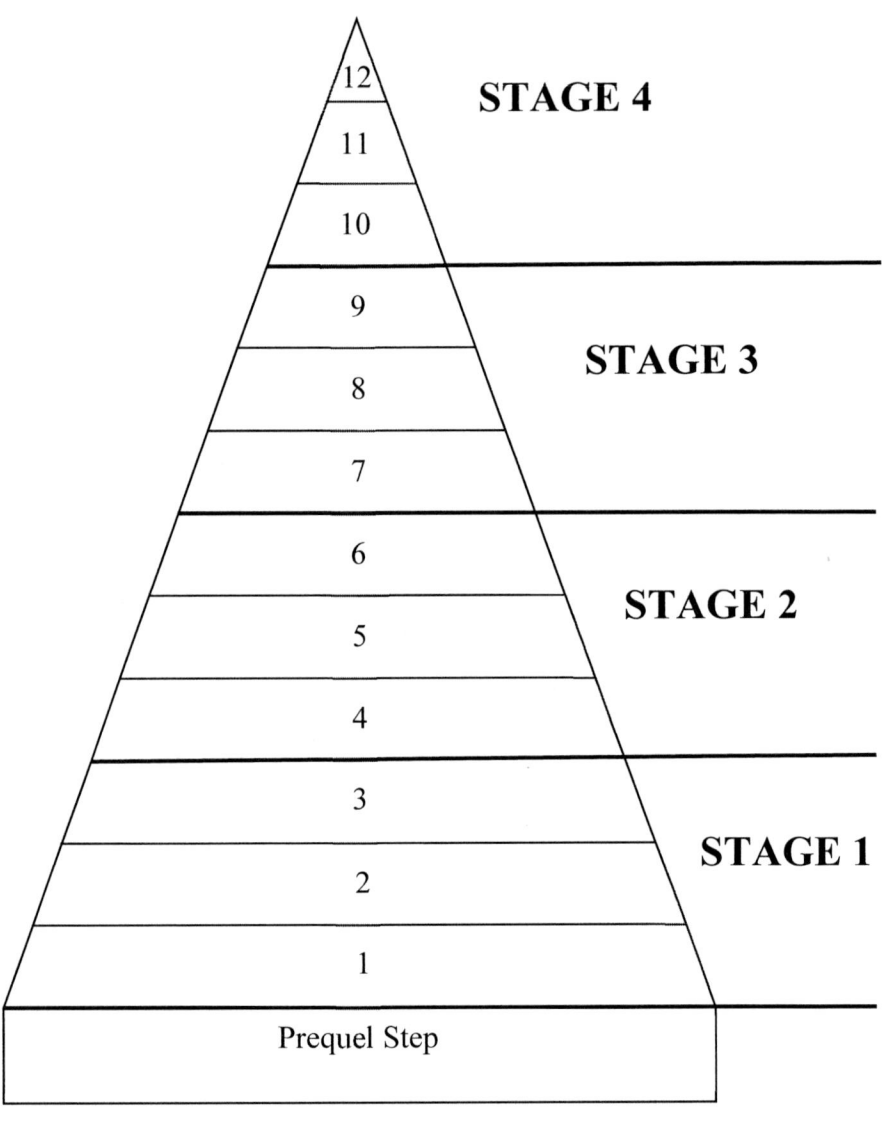

Figure 4: The twelve Steps and four Stages of Development on the Love Path.

[Designed by Imogen Bunting]

Siddhartha Gautama, better known as Buddha, taught a theory that requires each individual to take responsibility for their own enlightenment process. He passed on many pearls of wisdom to his followers, including the spiritual purposes of suffering and karma. Most importantly, through insight into his own psycho-spiritual evolution, he grasped the importance of the life, death and rebirth cycle of learning encapsulated in the process of reincarnation.

While other religious teachings together with academic studies in education, psychology and philosophy have also contributed to my ideas, it's obvious that the teachings of Jesus Christ and Buddha have coloured my emotional as well as my intellectual perception of what constitutes great love. And great love, rather than ordinary love, is what I imagine many of us aspire to. You will realise by now that I refer to great love as Christ-conscious love. Where my theory differs from earlier gnostic teachings is that I don't separate the physical from the spiritual. So when I refer to Christ-conscious love I am including sexual intelligence, whether we choose to be sexually active in our current incarnation or not.

The Love Path is comprised of four stages of maturational growth which we must pass through if we wish to attain the goal, Master of Love. I have classified these stages as: Kindergarten, School, University and Transfiguration. Each stage is comprised of three steps and is associated with a major theme of love development: sensuality, sexuality, advanced intimacy and Christ-consciousness. Figure 4 links the relevant steps to each stage of love development.

The inspiration for a four-stage process of psycho-spiritual development came from a seed sowing parable attributed to Jesus. The parable I'm referring to can be found in the Gospel of Luke 8:4–8, the Gospel of Matthew 13:1–9, and in the Gospel of Mark 4:1–9. In the story we are told that a farmer went to scatter seeds in a field. Some seeds fell on the nearby road and were eaten by birds or were stepped on. Other seeds landed on rocky ground and started to grow but died through lack of water. Other seeds fell among thorn bushes and began to grow well but were later chocked by weeds growing around them. The remaining seeds fell on good soil where they grew and produced a hundred times as many seeds.

The seeds scattered by the farmer symbolises wisdom. The ground represents our intelligence, firstly to recognise the seeds as being important, then to successfully germinate the ideas into our behaviour and then finally to nurture our psycho-spiritual well-being all the way to harvesting. Harvesting our own seeds of wisdom to help others is the final stage of growth.

Another seed sowing parable supports the proposition that gaining wisdom takes time. In the Gospel of Matthew 13:24–25, Jesus likened the kingdom of heaven to a farmer scattering good wheat seed in a field. While everyone is sleeping, an enemy invades the farmer's property and scatters weed seed over the top of the cultivated field. The good wheat seed represents true wisdom which is wholesome food for the mind, soul, body and heart, whereas the enemy's weed seed represents all the deceptions and temptations likely to choke growth, produce a false harvest and promote disease.

This second parable highlights a fundamental truth that the quest for knowledge is not easy. True wisdom and false wisdom grow side by side. It takes a lot of life experience and many incarnations, to separate the two. We can take heart from another biblical clue that when we do recognise true wisdom and act on it, we feel lighter and freer inside. This sensation of growing internal freedom is synonymous with expanding Christ-consciousness. As Jesus promised, the truth does indeed set us free.

Ascending the Pyramid of Wisdom is a personal journey and we do not need to critically assess the progress of others. The Zen principle of making no comparisons is useful in this context. In the Osho Zen Tarot, the card identified as the 5 of Clouds elaborates this idea very well. The teaching suggests that we shouldn't compare bamboo and oak, by saying that one plant is more beautiful or the other more valuable because both plants are special in their own way. And if we use this analogy with the psycho-spiritual development of humans, we can see that nobody is superior, and nobody is inferior, because everyone is incomparably unique. This is also true for our choice of developmental paths. The Love Path is not superior nor inferior to the other three paths that make up the Pyramid of Wisdom. Each path is unique and special in its own way.

Daily life on earth can be a competition. Not only do we compete as individuals for parental love, the best mate, the best grade, the best job, positive attention from friends and colleagues and to win at sport and games of all kinds, but we also compete for water, food, land, mineral resources, intellectual property, material goods, wealth, power and prestige. Competitiveness is ramped up in collective terms when it is expressed between families or groups within communities, between communities within nations and ultimately between nations on the global stage. Without shared agreements to live co-operatively, that is the reality of life on earth. It is therefore reassuring to know that the spiritual race to achieve Christhood and enlightenment is not a competition between people. The only person we compete with, is ourselves.

The model of love development displayed in Figure 4 represents this personal competition as a twelve-step stairway to heaven, or put another way, the evolutionary unfolding of our true natures as we make progress towards self-actualisation and Christhood. When we have ascended the twelfth step of the Love Path and completed all our maturational learning, we can call ourselves masters of love.

It is interesting that I constructed a four-stage model after studying Judeo-Christian literature and the mythology of the Holy Grail quest. Other theorists have arrived at similar conclusions. Hindu philosophy proposes four life stages and four goals of life, Buddhist teaching proposes four stages of development before achieving enlightenment and C G Jung advocated that the four stages of medieval alchemy are symbolic of personal growth needed to reach the ultimate goal of Individuation – 1. Blackening 2. Whitening 3. Reddening and 4. Yellowing.

Because love development is learned and is not determined by our biological age, the chronological sequence provided with my model is a theoretical guide only. We ascend the Pyramid of Wisdom in our own timing and in our own unique way. To give you an example, an individual could be fifty years old, wealthy, good-looking and successful in the corporate world yet have only reached kindergarten in terms of psycho-spiritual development. At the other end of the continuum, a highly evolved soul may have chosen to be born with severe disabilities to provide others with opportunities to love more deeply. In this latter case, the individual will radiate loving compassion from birth.

Finally, I want to explain why I chose a twelve-step design for my model. After several attempts using the sacred numbers 7, 11 and 22, I finally accepted the argument of the astrologer, Linda Goodman, that the twelve sun signs of the zodiac represent the 12 initiation stages of love. I renamed Goodman's stages as steps, included an additional step without numeric value and altered the descriptions of love tasks. Despite the alterations and the reworking of certain concepts, I agree with much of Goodman's theory and especially her argument that love development incorporates teaching as well as learning.

Stage One
Kindergarten: (Sensuality)

A belief in re-incarnation alters the way we view human birth. Evidence suggests that as we become more self-aware, we increasingly become involved in the process of our own evolving soul personality. We become more pro-active in choosing our new life circumstances and we begin to knowingly accept some difficulties to progress psycho-spiritual goals of development. We can conclude that what takes place before birth is highly significant, though at this stage of our theory building we are having to rely on subjective evidence, such as accounts of past-life flash backs, near death experiences and channelled psychic messages from spirit guides and deceased loved ones.

The idea that pre-birth planning sets the scene for a new human life experience fits well with William Glasser's Choice Theory. He argues that almost all human behaviour is self-chosen as it based on internal motivations. In the context of human evolution, we can see how these motivations have matured through millennia according to Maslow's theory of needs. Motivations to know more, to love better and to achieve more have been assisted by many evolutionary factors, especially education and advanced understandings of human and animal rights.

Underlying intelligent human decision-making is consciousness. Our early ancestors reacted to external stimuli through their senses. And the senses remain our primary mode of making meaning from experience in our earliest years. Our ability to make use of this experience creatively is given huge impetus with the acquisition of language, which allows us to reflect on the past and speculate on the future.

The evolution of the brain in ancestral humans is mirrored in the process of our own brain formation early in life. There are three distinct areas of the brain which represent phases of development: reptilian, limbic and neocortex. The first and therefore the most basic is the brainstem which is responsible for the involuntary system including sex. The limbic is the next stage of development and forms the subcortex. This is a more chemically active part of the brain as it manages emotional activity based on sensory information including movement, touch, taste, smell, pleasure and pain. The last part of the brain to develop is the neocortex area or cerebral cortex which is responsible for logical thought and speech. This is the last of the three areas to become fully activated and its efficiency is largely dependent on limbic brain development.

Learning to love is assisted by the individual process of reincarnation and by evolutionary change occurring in human brains generally. As our consciousness expands, we become more aware of our motivations and concomitantly the multiplicity of options facing us.

The proposition that we can choose to stay connected to those we love over many lifetimes makes sense of the phenomena we call soul mates. Individuals can use this opportunity to experience happiness or to promote evolutionary love development. But that is not the only way we expand our love understandings. We may decide to be born about the same time as people we have previously hurt or wronged in some way so that we can cancel our karmic debt to them. Evidence also suggests that we may choose to experience different cultures, roles, careers, and sexual identities in our quests to become more knowledgeable.

Like Deepak Chopra, I believe coincidences are purposeful and form part of our synchro-destiny. They provide us with clues about who we are and can confirm for us we're on the right path. This is particularly true in relation to falling-in-love, careers, friendships and odd meaningful encounters with strangers. We set the scenes for the likelihood of coincidences occurring before we are conceived. That we don't remember this after we are born ensures the mystery and the adventure of life is retained. For there is no way of demonstrating the acquisition of knowledge and the development of advanced attitudes and behaviours unless we're tested in new and unfamiliar situations.

We can only speculate about the preparation that takes place before we begin a new life, though we are continuing to collect snippets of information from many sources. For instance, one psychic message about a deceased partner of mine described him spending time in the healing rooms when he first crossed over because of trauma in his early life. Although the medium didn't know his personal story, she was right about the early life trauma. My partner had been born an illegitimate baby in England before the Second World War and was raised by his grandmother. During our time together, this partner described having to defend himself at school against name-calling and bullying. Another channelled messaged from a different psychic told me I'd chosen my life path before birth. My theory is that the options presented to us increase and become more varied as we develop psycho-spiritual intelligence.

No matter where we are in our psycho-spiritual evolutions, we all have guardian angels watching over us and spirit guides are variously assigned to us during our time on earth. In addition, we can access other angels and spirit guides if we choose to approach them for help and guidance. Richard Webster, Doreen Virtue and Diana Cooper have been useful writers for me on this subject but there are many other informed authors available.

Some esoteric clues are deftly hidden in the fields of astrology and numerology. I found Edmund Harold's book, *Master Your Vibration* particularly helpful because it doesn't sugar coat the effort required to reach self-actualisation. Harold suggests that our names and birth dates maybe salient indicators of pre-birth planning. If this is correct, it demonstrates how complex the evolution of individual difference really is.

The final word I want to say on the pre-birth stage of our development is that love comes in many colours. An individual may choose to undertake a very brief incarnation, such as the experience of being an aborted foetus or an infant who dies early, for their own spiritual development or to help those they love on earth to have opportunities for learning. Both Jesus and Buddha stressed the need for us to master suffering if we wish to find the keys to heaven and enlightenment. From this perspective, no experience is wasted, however hideous or hurtful, if it brings us closer to our true natures and therefore closer to God.

Step One
Infancy – Affection
(Attachment Versus Rejection)

Infancy on the Love Path schema is the period from birth until two years of age. A psychospiritual approach to human development accepts the impressive body of scientific findings already accumulated. For this reason we will begin our discussion of love development in Infancy with a brief look at attachment theory which has been widely researched.

John Bowlby's seminal work in the mid-twentieth century investigated the attachment process of human babies with their mothers. Following Bowlby, there was a flurry of projects that examined the attachment process from a wider perspective to include fathers, other primary caregivers, toys and special objects. Researchers, such as Michael Rutter, produced convincing arguments to discredit aspects of Bowlby's earlier research. Nevertheless, despite some obvious researcher biases and methodological problems, Bowlby can be credited with bringing to our attention the critical importance of attachment in a baby's early development. If the attachment process doesn't occur, or is incomplete, or is inconsistent, we can predict there will be consequences for later emotional development.

Because humans have evolved social personalities increasingly dependent on their families and communities for survival and wellbeing, attachment provides us with a sense of belonging. However, as no attachment process is perfect, we all experience to greater or lesser extents moments of feeling rejected. Fear of rejection and abandonment therefore remain potent subconscious motivations for most of us during the first three stages of psycho-spiritual development, particularly so if the attachment process during our first few years of life is unstable or interrupted in some way.

Since Bowlby's time, medical science has gathered evidence that the new-born's opportunities for well-being are improved if the health of the mother during pregnancy is well supported. And from social psychological research, we better understand how a myriad of other factors can assist the new-born's ability to grow and thrive, such as the mental wellbeing of caregivers, environments free of violence and abuse, clean water and nutritional food, intellectual stimulation and positive social interactions.

Many early life problems and deprivations have the potential to be healed and compensated for later in life if the individual is given the opportunity to experience consistent and dependable loving care, either informally through personal relationships or formally through emotional attunement and careful psychological mirroring in therapeutic relationships. Positive outcomes are more likely when the individual is highly motivated and already possesses some evolved self-awareness. However, despite the potential for healing later in life, some early life deprivations and attachment traumas result in permanent emotional damage.

Bowlby argued that permanent emotional damage leads to 'Affectionless Psychopathy' which is characterised by lack of concern for others, lack of guilt and an inability to form meaningful and lasting relationships. Other research findings have gone further and included addiction to sensory stimulation, abusive and violent behaviour, difficulty recognising their own feelings, inability to accurately assess the feelings of others and impaired social maturity.

Sometimes events intervene so that a baby is orphaned or the natural parents are unable to care for the child. If there are good enough substitute sources of love willing to provide emotional care and material protection, the baby can prosper. Humans have amazing potential for resilience and love can be learnt from many different sources. So, while two biological parents providing a nurturing start for a baby may be the mythologised cultural ideal, it doesn't follow that this scenario is essential for later love development.

I now want to shift the discussion to Jean Piaget's research on cognitive development. Although some contemporary commentators consider Piaget's work out of date because it's culturally biased and doesn't address the effects of modernisation and technology on brain function, I found his theories useful as a basis for explaining the early developmental stages of human love intelligence.

Piaget defined infancy as the Sensorimotor Stage of cognitive development which spans the period from birth to two years. This is the stage when we are discovering the relationships between sensations and motor behaviour. Piaget concluded the major cognitive task of infancy is mastery of object permanence. For example, young babies will not look for a toy that falls beyond their reach. However, about the age of eight months there is a change. The baby will search for a toy if it falls from view. Piaget argued that infants learn to distinguish between various objects and experiences and then form generalisations about them. This early cognitive development lays the groundwork for later intellectual and emotional growth.

From a psycho-spiritual perspective, the task of attachment is complicated. Not only do we need to bond with our new parents and caregivers to survive, but we also need to loosen our invisible connections to the psychic world we've come from to join the global human family. And becoming a member of a specific family, in a specific community and culture, requires us to recognise we have an independent identity not shared by our parents and caregivers.

From the moment we breathe our first breath we have begun the process of growing our own special social identity, in Jungian terminology our persona. Our persona attaches itself to our ego which has been with us from our original spiritual creation. Together they allow our conscious reality to survive in the constantly evolving world of objective reality.

Some of us take considerable time to complete our transition from the psychic world of our spiritual ancestry. It's not uncommon for pre-schoolers to maintain intermittent communication with angels and other spirit entities. Some highly evolved souls don't lose their connections to the spirit world completely but learn ways to manage them discretely within the mainstream objective culture. The easiest way of doing this is by incorporating imaginative and spiritual elements into creative play.

Donald Winnicott proposed that the child is born with a true self, which is the inherent personality, and a false self, which is largely socially created. Winnicott's argument fits well with the theory that we choose our parents and life goals before conception and then lose awareness of this in the birthing process. Like Deepak Chopra and many others, I believe it's a lifetime task to uncover our potential by remembering who we truly are and what we are primarily on earth to learn or achieve.

Linda Goodman suggests the first love initiation is governed by the sun sign Aries and is characterised by the statement 'I am'. She says the lesson to be learnt is that love is trust and that the teaching for others is that love is innocent.

I agree with Goodman's assertion that trust in others and a recognition of oneself as an independent human being are important psycho-spiritual tasks on the first step of development. However, I regard them as common tasks for all four pathways up the Pyramid of Wisdom. I believe the additional task to be mastered on the first step of the Love Path is affection, first to receive it and then to give it. Affection can be described as warm feelings of fondness and tenderness. These feelings are demonstrated through smiles, touch, vocal sounds and loving language. Touching behaviour includes hugs, holding hands, non-sexual kisses, stroking, grooming and tickling. Affection forms the basis of all later expressions of reciprocal love and emotional intimacy. In terms of what they teach us, babies represent new hope, beauty and innocent purity. They awaken our hearts to unselfish love and teach us to care more.

Step Two
Early Childhood – Imagination (Approval Versus Disapproval)

Early Childhood is the second step in the Kindergarten Stage of the Love Path. This is the period in our lives when we consolidate the learnings of babyhood and move to what Jean Piaget has labelled the Preoperational Stage of cognitive development. According to Piaget's research, the Preoperational Stage of cognition lasts from two to seven years. On my schema, Early Childhood is approximated to last from two to six years.

The main characteristics of Early Childhood are our developing capacity to employ symbols, particularly in the acquisition of language and egocentric behaviour as we haven't yet learnt to put ourselves in other people's shoes. In terms of attachment theory, we now understand that our parents or primary caregivers have other responsibilities that may require time away from us. We are no longer anxious about temporary separations from our attachment figures and we are ready for more varied social interactions and adventurous play.

Whereas Infancy was all about physical growth and comfort, spiritual holding, emotional attachment and mastering the principle of object permanence, Early Childhood propels us into the enigmatic dichotomy of human relations – personal subjective consciousness versus shared objective awareness. At the heart of the problem is the potential clash of realities between the normal human drives to survive, thrive, belong, and be loved with the growing realisation of being a named personality possessing independent thoughts and motivations.

The enormity of finding oneself alive in a human body can trigger nightmares and mild anxiety in some highly sensitive young children. Others may project their vague fears onto external monsters and mythological villains. It is not surprising, therefore, in the existential totality of psycho-spiritual development, that getting the balance right between the internal subjective world of thoughts, intuitions, and feelings with the external objective world of shared symbols, concepts, rules and meanings begins young and is essential for long-term mental health and the likelihood of actualising one's potential in this lifetime.

From a psycho-spiritual perspective, the capacity to love is given an enormous fillip during Early Childhood through the development of imagination. Fantasy is the means whereby we learn to transport ourselves into other characters, times and places. Not only is this skill essential for the later development of empathy, but we also need at least some basic levels of imaginative thought to enjoy romance and intimacy in adulthood.

During Early Childhood we become fascinated by our names and membership of family and social units. We become possessive about our toys and special attachments and experiment with emotional boundaries. Although our emotional connections with peers may be fickle, we are generally ready to explore the art of creating friendship. Either with friends, siblings or on our own, we spend large amounts of time mimicking adult behaviour or rehearsing archetypal roles we aspire to achieve through fantasy and play. A rich tradition of mythology and folklore can assist the individual to master the second step of the Love Path.

In a parallel process to cognitive and emotional development, our physical dexterity and gross motor skills allow us to experiment with our bodies and practise new skills including balance and spatial awareness. For some genetically endowed individuals, early signs of exceptional sporting, athletic or dancing talent may be revealed. For all of us, unless we are disabled in some way, growing physical independence assists the flowering of the internal world of our imagination through the literal experience of fantasy play and social relationships. We are lucky if our imaginations are fed on a regular basis with fascinating books and age-appropriate media presentations. We are even luckier if we begin some formal tuition in art, drama, music or dance that alights our passions to learn and extends our abilities more quickly.

In sophisticated modern societies, it's easy to see how the evolution of human awareness has been assisted by laws prohibiting child labour and compulsory free education for all boys and girls. When circumstances allow, Early Childhood is the perfect training period in life when our personalities have opportunities for growth and experimentation. However, if circumstances conspire to shut down our inherent potential for imaginative play, or our unique personality is consistently bruised, there will be repercussions in the way we express love and intimacy in adult life.

As in the Infancy step of love development, emotional wounding during Early childhood can frequently be ameliorated, or even healed completely, later in life. But there are no guarantees. Young children are vulnerable and love development can be truncated or in rare cases blocked completely by adult behaviour and traumatic life circumstances.

The genesis of modern depth psychological theory began when practitioners in the field of mental health discovered links between presenting symptoms of adult pathology and early life trauma. A vast amount of research since then has shed light on many varied mental health issues that can blight people's lives. Indeed, the Diagnostic and Statistical Manual of Mental Disorders, which serves as a common reference for clinicians working in the field of mental health, is a comprehensive tome. A study of the various diagnostic categories reveals how vital it is to have early life emotional bonding and consistent nurturing to minimise the risk of later mental health problems, including the behaviours associated with personality disorders.

That said, let's return to the psycho-spiritual challenges facing us in Early Childhood. Young children are the embodiment of innocence and pure truth. As

Jesus of Nazareth so eloquently put it, we do not enter the kingdom of heaven unless we are prepared to change and be like little children [Matt 18:3–4; Mark 9:35–37; Luke 9:47–48]. Jesus wasn't exhorting us to behave childishly but to be like children in the sense of developing moral honesty, congruent behaviour and mental clarity. John A. Sandford points out that the image of a small child is used by Jesus to highlight our eventual goal of not wearing a false social mask to hide our true personality. When we are living in a congruent manner there are no splits between external behaviour and internal thoughts, feelings and intuitions.

Herein lies the rub. We begin life with the ability to see truth clearly and react honestly but that often doesn't get us what we want or help us survive in the complex society of human behaviour. The need to fit in and belong requires us to give up aspects of personal freedom and spontaneity and adopt culturally defined ways of behaving. It's then a long climb up the Pyramid of Wisdom to regain our essential personality and release the fullest expression of our spontaneous creativity.

Adults can assist our learning in Early childhood by teaching us it's normal to make mistakes. This learning can expand when adults we care about are prepared to be vulnerable and honestly admit their own shortcomings. In evolutionary terms, this developmental aspect of childhood is relatively new. Parenting models in the past, particularly those from the upper social classes in Western culture, tended to parent children from an emotional distance and used religion as a socialising agency. In our modern largely secular societies, we have been forced to bridge the moral divide between adults and children with more honesty. Our best love learnings are those demonstrated to us through experience. A further step of understanding is added when any adult we are emotionally attached to is able to model for us the healing power of honest apology and forgiveness.

How our parents, grandparents, siblings, teachers and other significant people in our lives use the powerful tools of approval and disapproval will greatly determine whether we learn to love ourselves. Acceptance and affirmation promote the growth of healthy self-esteem. And possessing a sound sense of self is crucial for the development of resilience when facing difficulties in life. In terms of love development, the way we learn to love others will be determined by the way we learn to love ourselves.

When a client in couple counselling is unable to articulate approval for their partner as a person even though they may be justified in disapproving specific attitudes and behaviours, it's possible that they didn't experience consistent approval themselves during Early Childhood. Eric Bern's *I'm OK and You're OK* theoretical model is a useful reference for clients who recognise early life emotional wounding and want to make changes going forward.

Linda Goodman suggests the second love initiation is governed by the sun sign Taurus and is characterised by the statement 'I have'. She says the lesson to be learnt is that love is forgiveness and the lesson to be taught to others is that love is patient.

While I agree with Goodman's overall assessment in general terms, I think love development during Early Childhood requires mastery of two specific tasks. Firstly, we need to experience unconditional love so that we feel okay about ourselves even when our behaviour is disapproved of. Secondly, we need the circumstances and encouragement to create fantasy. Learning to fantasise is a pre-requisite for developing empathy and compassion later in life. The teaching young children provide for others is that innocent love is without manipulation or guile.

Step Three
Middle Childhood – Kindness (Fairness Versus Injustice)

Middle Childhood is the third and final step in the Kindergarten Stage of development on the Love Path and approximates the period from six to nine years. It's a period of growth and consolidation.

Through much practice, physical skills are honed and social skills are broadened. We become more emotionally conscious of our place in the pecking order of various hierarchies, such as family, school, sport, cultural activities and friends. Not only do we encounter new levels of competition in all areas of endeavour, but we are also likely to receive personal feedback about our appearance, personality traits, and popularity or otherwise.

During Middle Childhood, our ability to reason takes a giant leap. According to Jean Piaget's research, between the ages of six and eight years we master the ability he referred to as Conservation of Quantity. Younger children are generally unable to grasp the idea that a half-filled large squat glass may carry the same amount of liquid as a small narrow glass that's filled to the top. However, by Middle Childhood we can work out similarities and differences with more perceptual understanding and we are ready to solve much more complex problems. Piaget's asserted that around seven years of age we move to the Concrete Operations stage of cognitive development. Concrete operations functioning is associated with rational reasoning and logical operations in various areas of the curriculum, especially mathematics.

The thrust of this growth and new learning has an impact on our psycho-spiritual development. We are influenced by stories, whether real or fictitious, with increased understanding. We can identify heroes and villains by their motivations and recognise typical behaviours of each. Closer to home, in our own families and communities, we are learning which behaviours are considered socially acceptable and those which are frowned upon or even considered illegal. Our ability, or inability, to manage time constraints, moods and social behaviour will have consequences in the way we relate with others. Most of us learn that the rewards for fitting in with adult authority far outweigh the possible benefits of rebellious freedom.

One area of love behaviour that is given an obvious boost is our ability to share. This is not to say that we weren't tutored to do so earlier in life. Just that, now, we are able to comprehend the concept at a deeper level and realise that sharing is fair in principle. We also are gaining the cognitive ability to form rationales for societal values. While we don't possess the personal experience of a teen, we begin to recognise when principles are being violated both in the personal world of our own relationships and in the wider context of human affairs outside home and school. If we are developing a robust conscience and our emotional intelligence has been nurtured well, we will be forming personal generalisations about the injustices we see, either directly through experience or indirectly through various media.

Some children don't receive consistent loving care and some children have to cope with chaotic home circumstances. For them, learning love skills and attitudes is likely to be difficult. Indeed, by this age some unfortunate children will have already learnt that falsehood and deception can help them achieve success and popularity while protecting their vulnerable egos. They may have learnt that aggressive and sneaky behaviour can result in a sense of power which may also be admired by some of their peers. Whether these children learn to be overt bullies or more underhand manipulators, they are in danger of expanding their personas at the expense of their inherent intuitive inner worlds.

This is not to say that all children who experience a paucity of loving care and attention or suffer severe emotional trauma are doomed to be underhand, naughty and social misfits. Some individuals master early trials and tribulations with maturity beyond their years. I would argue that differences in individual responses can be explained by pre-birth soul personality evolutions. Even at this early stage of life, gaps are appearing between those who are developing a moral compass and those who aren't. And a pre-requisite for love development is a growing workable conscience.

The major love task of Middle Childhood is to develop the capacity for kindness. The acquisition of this knowledge and how it is applied in real terms is facilitated by an emerging interest in the establishment of rules and fair play. The difficulty the child is faced with is balancing a natural drive to succeed in a competitive environment alongside growing awareness that life in many ways isn't fair. It's understandable that this is a period of questioning rules and seeking answers to puzzling life situations. Progress is helped by having the emotional security of defined behavioural boundaries, and by adults who model natural justice and take the time to explain how we can still practice fairness in an unfair world.

On step three of the Love Path, the parable that Jesus told his followers about the Good Samaritan is likely to appeal to the altruistic aspect of our developing personalities. The parable shows us the practicalities of expressing neighbourly love. For those interested in ancient texts, the Old Testament also mentions the need to love our neighbours as ourselves.

As recounted in the Gospel of Luke [10:25–37], the story of the Good Samaritan tells of a Jewish man travelling to Jericho who is ambushed by thieves along the way. The traveller is stripped, beaten and left for dead at the side of the road. First a priest and then a Levite pass by. But both men ignore the injured traveller. Then a stranger from a different culture, a Samaritan, comes along and stops to offer first aid to the injured man. After cleaning and bandaging the traveller's wounds, the Samaritan puts the man on his donkey and transports him to a nearby inn. Next day, after making the traveller comfortable, the Samaritan departs leaving money for the injured man's recovery.

The message of the parable is that the stranger behaved like a neighbour and saved the injured man's life. Jesus argued that disciples of love need to aspire to this level of social awareness. We will explore a psychologically deeper meaning of the parable in step eleven.

For now, the important point I am making is that Middle Childhood is an ideal time to be exposed to inspiring tales of kindness. We will not grow to be kind to ourselves in adulthood, nor kind to partners in marriage, if we don't learn the rudiments of kindness when young. All three steps that make up the Kindergarten Stage of love development are essential for advanced emotional intimacy in adulthood, including kindness.

While fictional stories and real-life examples are useful learning tools, the capacity to be kind is made relevant by being involved in practical assignments. Whether through school or family, it's an ideal time to foster care of animals, nature and the environment. We can also teach children how to be charitable to people in less fortunate circumstances. Our understanding of kindness is greatly helped if parents, teachers and other significant adults are kind to us.

Linda Goodman suggests the third love initiation is governed by the sun sign Gemini and is characterised by the statement 'I think'. She says the lesson to be learnt is that love is feeling and the teaching for others is that love is awareness.

While Goodman's analysis is useful, I believe the major love task to be learned in Middle Childhood is how to be kind. Children at this level of development remind us that justice and fairness are important concepts in all areas of life on earth.

Stage Two
School: (Sexuality)

A move from the Kindergarten Stage of love development to the School Stage may feel normal or very unusual depending on age and circumstances. I will continue this discussion with reference to the hypothetical timeline of the Love Path, as shown in Figure 4, with the understanding that adults in therapy choosing to retrace this period of their lives for psychospiritual healing may find the process emotionally painful.

A move upward to the School Stage is accompanied by a heightened sense of self-awareness.

When we were younger, we used sensory information in a wholistic way to learn and thrive. Now our increasing ability to reason allows us to filter, interpret and store information systematically to allow homeostasis – metabolic equilibrium – to proceed. We are finally letting go our original childish innocence as our needs for survival and desires for happiness propel us into social acceptance within our cultural communities, where good and evil flourish side by side.

In the Kindergarten Stage we learnt to protect our vulnerable egos from time to time through various defensive behaviours such as: suppression of memory, dissociation, withdrawal, passivity, acting out and fantasy. However, if we've been pursuing any of the developmental paths up the Pyramid of Wisdom, we won't have permanently adopted a false mask to disguise evil intent or used deception in sustained and deliberate ways.

As humans we are all vulnerable to sin and error. Sin involves conscious evil whereas error does not. Young children may make a lot of errors but are generally free of sin. This is the reason why the move from the Kindergarten Stage of development to the School Stage is a major shift in awareness. We become increasingly aware of guilty feelings if we contravene learned rules about right and wrong and learned moral values about goodness and evil.

The promotion to School Stage of love development increases the likelihood that we will have more freedom to make choices for ourselves outside parental control. Along with some exuberance engendered by this new level of responsibility is the disquieting experience that not all decisions are easy to make. Perhaps the most obvious changes and challenges arrive with our developing sexuality. Besides adapting to the physical changes of puberty, we will also be learning to protect our egos through increasingly sophisticated coping mechanisms.

Life is increasingly complicated and we are learning the rules of the social game. Unfortunately, it's easy to learn to be expedient at the expense of our consciences, especially if we want to avoid negative outcomes like punishment, ridicule and social isolation. And to add to the potential confusion our social worlds are generally expanding. The chorus of approvers and disapprovers has grown and our peer group is rapidly gaining influence. This pattern of ramping up choices every time we reach a new level of self-awareness is maintained throughout this stage and the next one. Recent technological advances in social media have added time pressures to the mix.

As we leave behind the innocent sensuality of childhood, we are confronted with our emerging sexuality in exciting and terrifying ways. We cannot return to a state of blissful ignorance without adopting a religious life, retreating from social contact or going insane. The only way forward if we want to live life to the full is to change and grow.

An emphasis on mastering sexual skills in safe and responsible ways, as well developing the attitudes and behaviours that foster emotional love, is specific to the Love Path. While individuals on the other paths of the Pyramid of Wisdom aid world progress in many important ways, the contributions made by querents on the Love Path are essential for human happiness. We use our care and expertise to ameliorate and heal the suffering of others; we use our natural gifts and generosity to teach the young; we foster affection and kindness formally and informally by our own behaviour; we are confident in our sexual identities and can support others to express their true passions; and through our creative flair we add colour and style to our culture's social milieu in fashion, design (including tattooing), food and beverage preparation and in the aesthetic and performing arts. Followers of the Love Path have much to offer. To do this well, we have much to learn.

Step Four
Late Childhood – Empathy (Sensitivity Versus Insensitivity)

Late Childhood is the first step in the School Stage of love development and occurs theoretically between the ages of nine and eleven. While it covers a relatively brief period, it has enormous implications for our later abilities to love well.

Some girls may have already begun the growth spurt that heralds the beginning of the puberty process and have developed breast buds. During Late Childhood most other girls will also begin this pubescent growth process. Although boys generally are a little older than girls when they begin the five Tanner stages of masculine maturational change, they too will begin growth spurts during the years of Late Childhood. Along with the physical changes triggered by sex hormones, both genders will make cognitive advances that will allow the processing of information with more conceptual understanding.

In terms of love development, the major task to be mastered in Late Childhood is empathy. While younger children may show signs of empathetic behaviour, true empathy requires congruent mirroring of emotions with some sophisticated thinking. We have to understand our own thoughts and feelings sufficiently to imaginatively interpret the thoughts and feelings of others with sympathetic comprehension. Some children born with an abundance of sensitivity will master this step reasonably easily. Others may struggle a bit. However, if their intentions are on track, they too can learn to be empathic. If we don't master the attitudes and skills of empathy when young, we will inevitably have problems with advanced intimacy in adulthood.

Practical experience is the best way to develop love skills. We can raise the sensitivity quotient in most youngsters through judicious teaching methods and with an enlightened curriculum. Communication skills that embody empathic listening can be taught as well as body language that reflects empathic motivations. Nothing needs to be over complicated or over analysed. The object of the teaching is to familiarise the student with useful information and a basic skill set to deal with difficult, sad and extraordinary situations. These situations may be as varied as personal, family, school, community or the plight of species that share this earthly habitat with us.

Empathy is a challenging love skill to master because it requires us to consciously open our hearts and feel genuine sympathy for the suffering of others, both human and animal. In doing so, we deliberately put aside self-interest and focus on the needs of others. Empathy is the healthy side of unselfishness. Unfortunately, there are ways that unselfishness can be psychologically unhealthy or even pathological, such as when children decide to be compliant out of fear of adult reactions including physical violence, or when children are taught to put adult needs before their own for emotional, sexual or religious control.

So, while I advocate the practical teaching of *love skills*, I'm aware they are only tools. Skills can be used or misused depending on an individual's motivations. Taught well, love skills assist our ability to self-reflect and lay the groundwork for a deeper appreciation of happiness in adult life.

The early stirrings of puberty signal a change in our self-conscious understanding of sensual pleasure. Besides any objective information we may have gathered about sexuality, we are confronted with the erotic nature of love in a personal way through the hormonal changes taking place in our bodies. For those who have been victims of rape and childhood sexual abuse, the onset of puberty is likely to be complicated and possibly traumatic. It's understandable that the Love Path may not be the chosen route for now. However, like anyone, victims can revisit the Love Path later in life for emotional healing.

Entering Late Childhood on the Love Path is like being thrown out of the Garden of Eden. No matter how much information we have at our disposal, we are thrust into the puberty process whether we feel ready or not. The Eden myth therefore provides a useful analogy which is why I will offer you a modern interpretation of that ancient story.

As told in the biblical book of Genesis, God [our archetypal Spiritual Mother and Father] created earth and all who live in it. Taken symbolically, not only is the god-energy androgynous, but Adam and Eve aren't two literal people but the representation of our own androgynous psycho-spiritual inheritance.

Each of us is born with an androgynous soul personality. This makes sense of why Eve is created from Adams's rib in the Hebrew version of the story while in an older Assyrian creation myth Adam is created from Eve. We can see the gender split being re-enacted in the authority figures in the story. The authoritative protective male God demands obedience from Adam and Eve and tells them not to touch the fruit from the Tree of Knowledge. Wisdom, or the female aspect of God, represented by the serpent, undermines this dictum and prompts Eve into new awareness by enticing her to bite into the fruit of Knowledge.

When Eve is offered fruit from the Tree of Knowledge, she appears to have a choice – to ignore the serpent and stay safe or to risk all and become knowledgeable. Of course, there really is no choice because the serpent has already given her the significant clue. If we, like Eve, wish to reach the Tree of Life and become immortal and god-like, we first need to eat the fruit of Knowledge which will open our eyes to both good and evil, including our sexuality.

The price of this new knowledge is that we are forced to leave the protection and abundance of the Garden of Eden and undertake the human experience which includes mortal death. We are then unable to return to the eternal bliss of the symbolic Garden of Eden until we have concluded our investigation of good and evil and are ready to complete the final stage of love development, Transfiguration.

To assist humans in their evolutionary journeys to become god-like and immortal, it's recorded in the Book of Genesis that God provided Adam and Eve with tools and clothing. A modern interpretation of these symbols is that tools represent the evolution of technology and science and clothing represents the evolution of arts in shared expressive terms and defensive coping mechanisms in personal psycho-spiritual terms.

Late Childhood represents the enormous step of leaving behind childhood and preparing for self-responsibility in new ways. Our goal is to acquire the knowledge and skills necessary to succeed in school and in the wider community beyond the school gate, all the while continuing to develop attributes that will assist our psycho-spiritual growth.

Linda Goodman suggests the fourth love initiation is governed by the sun sign Cancer and is characterised by the statement 'I feel'. She says the lesson to be learnt is that love is freedom and the teaching for others is that love is devotion.

My interpretation of the fourth love step is that it is dominated by the physiological changes of pre-adolescence. It's a short space in terms of linear time but a pivotal one in terms of developmental changes in all areas of the individual's life. I regard the important love task to be mastered is empathy. Older children can teach us to be more sensitive and have respect for individual differences. They inspire in us a devotion for the higher principles of life.

Step Five
Puberty – Idealisation
(Esteem Versus Shame)

Puberty is the second step of the School Stage on the Love Path. I have identified the puberty process as a special step in our love development because I wanted to emphasise the importance of reaching sexual maturation in our personality development.

By sexual maturation I am referring to the first menstruation for girls and the first ejaculation for boys. On the Love Path model, I have suggested that the process of puberty affects most of us between eleven and fourteen years. Although some early and some late developers won't fit within this chronological timeline, because we are all linked generationally to our peer group, we can say that this period in our lives is governed by the significant physiological change process of sexual maturation. We leave behind childhood and prepare ourselves for the teenage identity we have yet to assume.

Whether or not we've previously enjoyed the sensual sensations of our bodies in exploratory play, we are now capable of pleasuring ourselves to orgasm. Although masturbation was historically a taboo subject, today it is increasingly accepted as normal practice for both males and females of all ages. Consequently, girls lucky enough to be living in Western democracies now have access to information and toys unheard of several generations ago.

The art of loving requires us not only to become well-informed but to become confident through personal experience. Mistakes and unwise choices are much less likely to occur if we don't rely on partners to satisfy our normal human sexual drives. Being confident about our own bodies and how we like to be pleasured can assist gender equality in the bedroom with future partners and undoubtedly enhances mutual sexual satisfaction in long-term committed adult relationships.

The process of puberty is experienced within the framework of family, school and community. In recent times, young adolescents in Western society have much more information readily available to assist them on their journeys of knowledge, including sexual self-identification. However, although technology allows modern youth easier access to important information that is helpful, it also has the potential to open up a Pandora's box of unhelpful and even damaging sexual content that can lead to distorted attitudes and manipulative behaviours including sexual violence. It is therefore important that serious topics which foster safe and respectful sexual relationships are taught alongside the dangers of unwanted pregnancy; sexually transmitted infections; illegal pornography; sexual harassment, assault and rape; and the strategic use of alcohol and drugs by sexual predators of young people.

Even when adolescents receive the best available education about human sexuality, life can still be a painful teacher. It's important they have caring adults in their lives who provide sensible advice as well as nurturing and predictable emotional security. It's much easier to retain self-confidence when we know we are loved by our families especially when they demonstrate they still care for us when we make errors of judgement or behave badly due to hormone driven mood swings. Indeed, it is crucial for later adult happiness, that issues around our blossoming sexuality assist the growth of self-esteem and we are not left with pockets of secret shame.

Universal education, reliable contraception, changing social attitudes to virginity and marriage and the popularity of secularism have altered the way we view puberty in Western society. This evolutionary process has freed us to view puberty as a normal human process that is to be welcomed rather than feared. Adults can help by explaining that sexuality is like money, neither good nor evil just a normal facet of human life. Sex can be enjoyed without guilt if we don't contravene laws of the land or our own set of evolving moral principles.

Despite the excitement of perceiving sexual maturation as a sign we're growing up, it's common to experience some ambivalence during the process of puberty. This can result in feelings of uncertainty and inadequacy. Quite apart from physiologically induced hormonal swings, we can be subject to emotional highs and lows for psychological reasons. Our bodies and faces may alter in ways we don't like. Acne is an obvious example but there are many others such as noses growing out of proportion to the face, weight gains before growth spurts, girls' breasts being different sizes and boys' voices breaking at inconvenient times and places. Throw into the mix a desire to fit into a peer group of choice and the change process of puberty may activate some emotional stressors not encountered before.

The roller-coaster ride of pubescent emotions may be further complicated by sadness and regret – even if not articulated – for the childish innocence and spontaneous wonder being left behind. This sadness has the potential to turn into anxiety or episodic depression – either mild or more seriously clinical – if life becomes complicated. Situations likely to impede a smooth transition through Puberty are losses of all kinds including death and parental separation; accidents and disease; unhappy home situations including domestic violence; undeclared sexual abuse; material poverty; intergenerational low self-esteem; feeling bullied or socially isolated; traumatic incidents in the wider community whether triggered by nature or human actions; and being introduced into the adult world of sex, alcohol and other drugs prematurely and inappropriately.

Although we humans have amazing abilities to rise above trauma and difficulties, as young adolescents we are particularly vulnerable to feeling overwhelmed by situations outside our control. It's therefore very important we are well supported by families, schools and social services. To accept and love ourselves, we need to be proud of our sexuality and all that it represents.

For those of us who choose the Love Path with some spiritual awareness, Puberty may produce some inner conflicts that feel confusing. We may need to prioritise the construction of a secure social persona to protect our egos from unhelpful and even permanently damaging psychological bullying and ridicule. Personality traits that were considered sweet and disarming when we were very young may now appear socially gauche and unattractive. It's normal to want approval from friends and classmates. However, we may find that fitting in socially puts us on a collision course with our spiritual intuitions. The best advice I can give is that we may need to protect our secret worlds of spiritual contemplation, and enjoy going with the social flow. There are times to stand alone and there are times to rest in the collective warmth of the crowd. Let destiny light the way ahead when the time is right.

During Puberty, as in all stages of human development, it is inevitable we will make mistakes – that is what biting the fruit of experience entails. Errors often don't impact on future life choices, although in some cases mistakes can't be undone with tragic results. Accepting what can't be changed while retaining hope for a better future is an important learning step. Fortunately, we can be helped in this endeavour by seeking adult sources of wisdom who show us they care.

As Puberty is the door to adulthood maturity, it's an ideal time to gather stories of hope and redemption. They will assist the growth of love resilience. Love resilience is like having a spiritual insurance policy in case times turn rough. So, as well as finding singers, musicians, actors, sporting stars and other famous iconic personalities to be our transitional idols, we can idealise heroes of fiction and non-fiction who demonstrate how courage and well-intentioned action can make the world a safer and better place.

Linda Goodman suggests the fifth love initiation is ruled by the sun sign Leo and is represented by the teenager who needs to master the statement 'I will'. She says the lesson to be learnt is that love is humility and the teaching for others is that love is ecstasy.

I believe the major skill to be learnt on the fifth step of love development is idealisation. Idealisation requires us to recognise the qualities in others we want to emulate for ourselves. This is not a new idea. Sigmund Freud coined the expression ego ideal to describe the process of patterning ourselves on someone we hold in great respect or admiration. Idealisation provides the adolescent with maps to follow and inspires dreams of personal greatness. This skill, once learnt, can be useful in adulthood, especially in our choices of partners, friends and careers. And learning the skill during Puberty assists our search on the next step of love development when the task requires us to establish a self-defined personal identity.

I think the significant learning adolescents teach others is that we don't own them. They come into this world with their own unique soul personalities and psycho-spiritual heritages.

They won't always fit the templates of our expectations.

Step Six
Later Adolescence – Identity (Boundaries Versus Enmeshment)

We have reached the challenging step of Later Adolescence. Teenage love, as epitomised in Shakespeare's play, *Romeo and Juliet,* may appear forbidden, highly passionate and ultimately doomed, yet it's a rite of passage to be welcomed rather than feared. Even when our private devotion is bestowed on unattainable icons of good looks, personality, talent and fashion, we can relish this new erotic dimension to our lives as the harbinger of adult freedoms soon to be our own.

The love step of Later Adolescence on the Love Path schema characteristically occurs between fourteen and twenty years of age. Puberty has been completed and brain development is well advanced. According to Piaget's theory we have begun the final process of cognitive development he termed Formal Operational.

Piaget asserted that cognitive learning is achieved through the complementary processes of *accommodation* and *assimilation.* These terms can also be applied to learning the art of love. As love novices, we gather new information and accommodate it into our existing structure of knowledge. Sometimes new information comes directly through experience and sometimes indirectly through conversations, books, film, the internet and other media. We then use trial and error, practice, self-reflection and feedback from others to assimilate this new learning into the framework of our personalities, often in modified form. In some cases, we discard ideas that no longer fit into our developing value system or cease behaviours that we now deem to be childish.

Adolescence is a time of great change and progress. For some of us, it's also a time of new difficulty. This is especially so if we feel misunderstood by those we care about. We are extremely lucky if our parents practice unconditional love and have learnt how to disagree without rancour or negative judgements. For those of us who are loved but discover that the love we receive is accompanied by expectations that we will conform to family values we no longer believe in, the teen years can be stressful. My little piece of wisdom to questers on the Love Path is that patience can be a useful skill to master. We can quietly plan an overall strategy and fight our personal battles on a narrow front. By this I mean we can be selective about topics we want to discuss or dispute and be careful with our presentation.

If we meet with disapproval about the way we express our sexual identities, we may need to look for additional support outside our family. Older teens and young adults who've successfully navigated similar stormy waters are likely to be helpful, as too are counsellors outside the school system. Whatever course of action we take, it's useful to adopt a long-term view. This period of life will soon pass, and we will be free to follow our own precepts and lifestyle choices. If possible, we should avoid conflict and negative judgements that may jeopardise our plans for tertiary education or career aspirations.

For those of us who possess psycho-spiritual abilities that are feared or demonised by some people, we need to nurture our special gifts and consciously protect them. The temptation is to make dramatic and often ill-devised scenes to demand acceptance and affirmation. Unfortunately, this is likely to backfire and ramp up fear that we have completely lost the plot. Remember, if we are loved and understood we are likely to be supported. However, if we are loved but misunderstood, we are likely to have our personalities or behaviour, or both, pathologised in some way. As a teen, with little economic or political power, it's wise to focus on practical goals that will assist our transition to independent adulthood.

Jesus highlighted the benefits of youthful rebellion in his parable of the prodigal son (Luke 15: 11–32). The tale goes like this. There was a man who had two sons. The younger son was restless and asked his father for his share of the estate. The father divided his assets between his two sons and the younger one left for a distant land where he squandered his inheritance on high living. Just when he decided it was time to earn some money, the country suffered a severe famine and the only job he could get was feeding pigs. Half-starved and ill-kempt the young man reflected on his past and came to his senses. The hired help on his father's estate were much better off with plenty of food and good living conditions. He decided to travel home, beg his father's forgiveness and ask to be employed on his father's estate.

When the rebel son returned home, his father not only forgave him but was so thrilled to see him that he arranged a celebration dinner and welcomed him onto the estate as a son and heir. The older son, who, on the surface, had done all the right things, was unable to rejoice at his brother's return and was consumed with resentment and jealousy. The younger son, despite all his errors and sins, had learnt more about love and life than the older son who hadn't strayed from the predictable path of material comfort, social conformity and parental expectations.

In a later chapter we will return to the parable of the prodigal son and add some depth of understanding for mature living. However, for now, the parable reminds us to look at adolescent rebellion with an open mind. We don't easily discover who we are or how we want our lives to be by being passive observers or remaining enmeshed in family expectations. Learning to consider ourselves as independent personalities with our own hopes and dreams is an important existential task of Later Adolescence. We can practice the skill of boundary setting which will become increasingly important in later adult life.

Another example of interest to our discussion is Perceval, a young hero of the Holy Grail quest. Perceval leaves his mother against her wishes to become a knight in King Arthur's court. As he is one of the few who successfully reach the Grail, this early sign of defiance by Perceval is later shown to be the correct course of action.

As a young quester on the Love Path, we can help ourselves by keeping alive our secret aspirations and learning about life from established sources of wisdom. Let's take the Greek myth of Narcissus as an example. Narcissus was a young hunter renowned for his beauty. However, he was proud and arrogant towards all who fell in love with him. When Narcissus rejected all the suitors without empathy or compassion, Nemesis, the goddess of retribution, arranged for him to fall in love with his reflection in a pool of water. He then died in despair because he was unable to possess the object of his love.

The moral of the story is not that self-love is wrong but rather that self-awareness cannot develop if we focus exclusively on the on the external attributes of beauty and ignore what is required to develop beauty within. Not only does this truism apply to us, but it also makes the process of choosing partners and friends interesting and potentially educational.

Due to Sigmund Freud's interpretation of the pathology he labelled narcissism, there is a tendency to label people as narcissistic indiscriminately without understanding the spiritual basis of self-love. According to Edward F. Edinger, to fall in love with one's reflection is an indication of an alienated ego. I would agree and argue further that to fall in love with one's own reflection demonstrates no conscious connection to the Christos at all. We can liken this level of psycho-spiritual evolution to the seeds that fell on the barren ground in the Jesus parable. Narcissus hadn't mastered the first step of love development.

A true narcissist cannot handle criticism of any kind and cannot acknowledge their own errors and sins. They have difficulty celebrating the gifts of others and tend to view feedback as personal attack. It's not so much that their behaviours appear grandiose, as we can all be guilty of that, it's that their motivations can be vindictive and vengeful. Someone with a narcissistic personality disorder displays behaviours that are psychologically harmful and physically dangerous to others. If our self-love is matched with love for others, we aren't narcissists but free spirits trying to find our way home in a world that may misunderstand us.

The myth of Narcissus teaches us to go deep with our self-love and develop beauty within so that we can love others as ourselves. Self-love can include respect for our bodies and attention to our appearance as well as developing worthy personality traits. As teenagers, it's perfectly normal to be fascinated by dress, make up, hair, art and music. Experimenting with different roles and styles helps us establish our unique identity.

Linda Goodman suggests the sixth love initiation is governed by the sun sign Virgo and is characterised by the statement 'I analyse'. She says the lesson to be learnt is that love is fulfilment and the teaching for others is that love is pure.

I consider the important love task for Later Adolescence is to establish an independent identity. We can help ourselves do this by learning to set appropriate personal boundaries in relationships at home, at school and in the community. The important teaching for others is that teenagers hold the creative promise of things to come. They need encouragement from adults and increasing freedoms for their unique potentials to shine.

Stage Three
University: (Advanced Intimacy)

Progression to stage three on any path of the Pyramid of Wisdom is a major shift in psychospiritual development. In terms of the Love Path, readiness is dependent on the individual having integrated into their personalities the basic building blocks of love functioning across the modalities of thoughts, feelings, intuitions and sensations – including the sexual motivations we refer to as lust. We can therefore postulate that individuals completing stage two have already acquired a relatively sophisticated knowledge system which governs most of their behaviour and generally aligns with their current conscience formation.

The first six steps which make up the first two stages on the Love Path were sufficient evolutionary progress for much of humankind during past millennia. This is because a true intimacy is based on equality. Power imbalances in relationships skew the dynamics of open communication. Traditional marriage based on male dominance and privilege didn't prevent loving intimacy between marriage partners but did generally stifle personal quests to explore the nature of love with guilt-free freedom.

The emergence of individuality as a psychological construct may be as old as Jesus, but political, religious and economic conditions for most folk over following centuries did not support the flowering of personal love intelligences. Advanced love development was generally limited to small numbers of independently minded individuals who worked or thought creatively and were fortunate to have opportunities for varied life experiences.

Social advances over the twentieth century altered the love landscape. Coincidentally, just as we have evolved our knowledge and ability to love well the need for us to do so has risen in a parallel fashion. The current environmental, political and social problems facing the global human family will not be solved without an exceptional leap in evolutionary love development. For although artificial intelligence, deep learning and other scientific advances offer hope of better times to come, such progress won't be worth a brass razoo if hate, avarice, intolerance, injustice, inequality, corruption and religious fundamentalism distort how this new knowledge is applied.

Fortunately, the cumulative effects of social change interfacing with social media have resulted in young people today being better informed. Around the world there are discernible generational swings towards intelligent sensitivity. My contention is that increasing numbers of individuals are promoting themselves to stage three of the Love Path. Not only are overall numbers increasing but individuals are making conceptual gains more quickly. If this trend continues, my hypothetical timeline could well shrink in coming generations.

Linda Goodman, the astrologer who influenced the framework of my Love Path theory, lived her seventy years between 1925 and 1995. Her personal psychohistory inevitably influenced the writing of her seminal work *Love Signs,* which was first published in 1979. As I was born in 1946, a whole generation later than Goodman, it is understandable that my theory of evolutionary love development reflects a society more aware of what is required to achieve gender equality. I am more optimistic that people will consciously choose to grow more loving when they appreciate the benefits are worth the effort not only for themselves but for society as a whole.

Goodman argued that we need to complete the first six love initiations several times in different incarnations before we can progress to the second set of six. She then asserted that we need to repeat the second set of six love initiations several times before being gifted enlightenment. I'm not sure if her assessment is correct. My understanding is that anyone can complete the ascension of the Pyramid of Wisdom on any of the four paths of knowledge or on any combination of paths. The only requirement is that we need to master each step before we are promoted to the next. But I could be wrong. Given the emphasis Jesus of Nazareth placed on love development, it's possible that psycho-spiritual development remains incomplete until we master the art of loving.

Looking back over human history, we can identify markers of evolutionary love development through the lives of special teachers, cultural mythologies and the creative efforts of individual writers, poets, musicians, artists and courtesans. At various times groups formed into influential movements for change. In Western culture, collective attempts to express new ideas about love occurred at various times. For example, during medieval times emphasis was given to courtly love and chivalrous behaviour and themes of love were popular in the ballads of troubadours. Love themes were also common in the visual and expressive arts of the eighteenth-century Romantic movement which was a reaction to the intellectualism of the earlier enlightenment period. And closer to our own times, the jazz age of the roaring nineteen twenties propagated liberalism and a sensual approach to love. These ideas were picked up and expanded upon decades later during the anti-establishment flower power movement of the nineteen sixties and seventies which advocated making love not war.

While love movements have contributed to evolutionary progress, they have not been the only sources of psycho-spiritual change. The political and social advances of feminism, for example, are just as likely to have gained their impetus from individuals on the Truth, Peace and Warrior paths. We can therefore conclude that it is through prior evolutionary progress on all paths of the Pyramid of Wisdom that a new epoch of love development is now possible.

In stage three of the Love Path we will discuss the most important and relevant love challenges facing us in Early, Middle and Later Adulthood. We are now capable of understanding love at a deeper level because we have completed, or are in the process of completing, the final phase of our brain development. According to Jean Piaget, Formal Operational cognitive development allows us to think and reason with more abstract logic. We can muse on theoretical constructs, devise hypothetical scenarios, create counter factual inner worlds, strategise and plan with multifarious inputs and transfer conceptual learning from one set of circumstances and apply it to new untried situations.

As our ability to think matures, so too does our awareness of the many options available to us. According to theories of problem solving, we have two main ways of making decisions about best option choices: analysis and creativity. Having the freedom to choose our own options in life throws us into new levels of self-responsibility. In psycho-spiritual terms, we are now ready to sort the good wheat seeds from the bad weed seeds. This is an interesting phase of our lives when our innate spiritual potential can be robbed through inertia, addictions, stubbornness, fear, mental illness, misinformation, seducers and predators.

If we follow the Love Path, our perception of love is dominated by our emotional and sexual intelligences. Love is likely to be processed differently on other pyramidal paths. For example, on the Truth path, an interest in love will be largely filtered through the mind. Followers of truth may view love concepts through studies in social justice, law, media, politics, science and teaching. And they could very well find Lawrence Kohlberg's theory of moral development interesting.

So, while there will always be common principles between the various paths on the Pyramid of Wisdom at equivalent stages of development, perceptions of topics will differ between the adherents of different fields of knowledge. With this in mind, let's proceed with a discussion of the three steps that comprise the University Stage of the Love Path, which is governed by the theme of advanced intimacy.

Step Seven
Early Adulthood – Commitment (Negotiation Versus Manipulation)

Early Adulthood on the Love Path schema refers to the period from twenty years to thirty-two years. This is when we are establishing ourselves as individuals in the social hierarchies of our communities. We take the identity we achieved in Later Adolescence and attempt to find a good fit for ourselves in the speculative and competitive world of adult functioning.

Questers of knowledge on the Love Path are those of us primarily concerned with exploring the nature of love through the emotional language of our hearts. Much of the knowledge we have already accumulated will be personal to us. The major love task in Early Adulthood is to learn about commitment. This can quickly become an emotional balancing act as we prioritise needs for further education, career and financial security with the adventurous fun of travel or engaging in meaningful work to assist global change. The challenging aspects of commitment can be further ramped up if we become involved in a long-term relationship with a special partner or if we want to maintain strong emotional ties with individuals who don't have the approval of our family circles.

Commitment affects all areas of our lives. In earlier times, gender roles were defined and our understandings of commitment were largely determined by cultural traditions, religious tenets and social mores. The scientific, technological and social revolution of the twentieth century ushered in a new era of individual responsibility. While we've largely been liberated from the emotionally claustrophobic rules and expectations of the past, we've found the new freedoms have produced new stresses of their own. There is more uncertainty about what commitment means when relationships and careers are no longer set in stone and there is more fluidity and change throughout all our lives. Mastering the art of commitment is no easy task and occupies much of our love focus during Early Adulthood.

One of the obvious dreams to be given a death blow for young people of today is that marriage no longer guarantees life-long commitment. Without legal and religious sanctions to force people's behaviour, the fairy tale happily-ever-after scenario is no longer sacrosanct. Indeed, by Early Adulthood most of us understand that although good marriages have the potential to last until one partner dies, in modern Western society all marriages require dynamic participation if they are to succeed and bring happiness to both partners.

For most questers on the Love Path, finding the ideal partner is an important goal. We understand we may have many relationships before we find the special one, the partner we want to spend the rest of lives with. However, whether we are in a serious relationship or not, the meaning of commitment is important at a conceptual level. First, and foremost, we are committed to our own happiness and self-actualisation. Finding lasting love with another person maybe an important goal, but if we also want to develop self-awareness and self-worth, our love of another person cannot be at the expense of our own identity, self-respect and truth. This advanced view of commitment is, of course, much easier said than done. This explains why the process of mastering commitment generally takes many years.

Love attractions in Early Adulthood are often with individuals who hold different views and beliefs or who come from different backgrounds. Difference is sexy. These partners have much to teach us if we stay open to the learnings. The only thing we need to remember is that we don't have to do anything we don't want to nor commit to any relationship we have doubts about.

Besides having relationships with people who don't share our psycho-spiritual awareness, we can learn a lot from friends and partners who've chosen different paths on the Pyramid of Wisdom. We can't become masters of love without understanding and respecting the perspectives and qualities of folk on the other paths. The easiest way to gain this knowledge, without spending time on the other paths, is through our relationships with others. Partners and close friends offer us a bounty of insight, even if we don't mine it until later in life.

Commitment is the developmental task of Early Adulthood that allows us to grow our understanding of love. In addition to the gifts of insight we gain from others, we have our own swag of past learning to assist us. We know how to be kind, how to share, how to empathise, when to be affectionate and when to be sexy. Now we need to think about what we mean by commitment and then learn how to prioritise and balance competing personal desires for happiness with interpersonal and communal demands for our attention, energy, resources and time.

I now want to recount two little stories to illustrate how evolutionary change has altered our expectations of love and marriage within a relatively brief period of time. In the first example, we have a rags-to-riches story of a beautiful pure young maiden plucked from domestic service and obscurity to become the wife of a handsome prince who is heir to the throne of his kingdom. In this bewitching tale, there is a fairy godmother and magical events helping the heroine reach her destiny. Trying to stop her happiness are a tyrannical stepmother and three stepsisters ugly with jealousy and envy. Throw into the drama an enigmatic glass slipper and the notion that the heroine is not only fatherless but an orphan, and we realise this seemingly simple story holds a few esoteric secrets beyond a simple yarn to put children to sleep. The story finishes with the predictable wedding and we are told the prince and his princess live happily-ever-after.

Fast forward to the twenty-first century and we have a little story that illustrates changed gender roles and new openness to sexuality. It also demonstrates a substantial leap in our psycho-spiritual understanding of love's purpose. It goes like this. An accomplished violinist has finished practice with her city's symphony orchestra. On her way home, her attention is arrested by a busker who has the husky voice of a modern Don Juan. Our heroine manages a jazz band in her spare time and realises she has struck gold. She makes an offer the busker can't refuse. After a brief stint in rehab, a new wardrobe of clothes and the fun of sharing our heroine's luxurious inner-city apartment, the busker soon agrees to an engagement. He doesn't need much persuading as their sex life is both varied and passionate. Just before the wedding takes place, the jazz band are invited to perform for a party of entertainment executives. The busker, alone, is then invited to record his voice. This triggers a rapid rise to mega stardom. Marriage plans are put on hold while our hero pursues his dream. Unfortunately, a fanatical terrorist bombs the city stadium where the busker is performing.

Our heroine is left heart-broken, still single and childless, endlessly repeating to her therapist, 'It wasn't supposed to end like this! It wasn't supposed to end like this!' Many years later, our heroine, still single and childless, finds fame and fortune through composing heavenly music which has the power to bring audiences to tears. Eventually she finds committed love and happiness with a widowed conductor of orchestras who has two adult children.

These little tales illustrate the changing face of marriage and our increasingly sophisticated understanding of love. They also demonstrate that the spiritual purpose underlying events can often be difficult to comprehend. We are at risk of deep disappointment if we cling to unexamined and outmoded templates of happily-ever-after wedded bliss and forget to live fully in the present.

We enter adult relationships with emotional baggage from our family-of-origin experiences and other loves we've known along the way. If we've suffered any sort of sexual abuse of physical violence, there will also be special vulnerabilities that don't always surface in ways we'd anticipate. Similarly, early life losses such as death of a parent, parental separation or adoption can be reactivated by experiencing rejection, abandonment or disloyalty from current adult partners. The power of these old wounds was brought home to me forcefully in the counselling room when I concurrently had three male clients independently referred to me by doctors for erection problems. All three clients had been in committed relationships that had ended badly, had early life losses, had nothing physically wrong with them and now wanted to find lasting love. Although therapy took some time and varied in length according to three different unique psychohistories, each gentleman consciously chose to make some changes and regained normal sexual behaviour. And, very importantly, all happily embarked on new life stories with more understanding about themselves and the nature of love.

Couple commitment is assisted by both partners being sure of their intentions. For the first six to nine months of a relationship we are generally testing each other. Sometimes cupid's arrow flies so fast, partners are smitten in a uniform fashion and recognise early they've fallen in love. For many relationships it isn't that simple and the decision to commit is not made for one or two years into the relationship. We now come to the interesting topic of legal marriage. The push for a formal engagement is normal. Problems arise if one partner is keen and the other holds back. Sometimes the window of opportunity passes by. Why would we commit to someone if we can't trust their love for us? This is definitely the time to seek professional help. It will clarify the situation one way or the other.

Couple commitment can by eroded by taking too long to make changes or by individual needs for independence. Some compromise is usually needed. On the other hand, if independence is totally stifled, we are at risk of losing sexual passion and eventually the relationship itself. It's a balancing act that needs tact and understanding. We are more likely to stay together if each of us lets go something from the past – such as an old flame, close friendship or interest. It's like Moses being prepared to sacrifice his beloved baby son Isaac to demonstrate his love for God. Trust grows ten-fold when our partner makes a difficult decision in our favour. How commitment is handled in the early months and years will have long-term implications for trust building and respect. Fostering individuality within a secure loving partnership is a tricky process that can't be hurried or faked.

Learning how to commit is an important love skill that becomes easier with practice. Manipulation is more likely to occur when partners aren't honest with each other and aren't honest with themselves. Then emotional blackmail, moods, passive aggressive behaviour, controlling techniques, fibs, lies and all sorts of game playing become the order of the day. Learning to negotiate fairly allows individuality to thrive whilst enjoying the benefits of a deeply emotional and sexually passionate relationship.

Early Adulthood is the ideal time to reflect on the meaning of commitment. While any partner is likely to be high on our list, so too will be any children we have or want to have in the future. We will want to consider the importance of extended family members and friends. We may also want to reflect on our commitment to ourselves, our values, our interests, our ongoing education or other abstract ideas. A hierarchy of commitments, to be reviewed as circumstances change, is a useful way of keeping track of our own psycho-spiritual development.

Linda Goodman suggests the seventh love initiation is governed by the sun sign Libra and is characterised by the statement 'I balance'. She says the lesson to be learnt is that love is harmony and the teaching for others is that love is beauty.

My interpretation of the seventh love step is that commitment is the major challenge to be understood and internalised. The associated skill set to be mastered is negotiation. Learning to negotiate fairly and honestly in love relationships based on equality requires an advanced level of communicating. We can learn these skills by observing others we admire or by attending couple workshops or therapy. The step seven teaching for others is that committed partnerships based on love have boundaries that need to be respected by other admirers.

Step Eight
Middle Adulthood – Loyalty (Respect Versus Disrespect)

Middle Adulthood on the Love Path schema occurs approximately from thirty-two years to forty-four years of age. This is the second step of the University Stage of love development and continues to be governed by the theme of advanced intimacy. Whereas the focus of the previous step was internalising the process of commitment and becoming more confident about negotiating differences that arise in our significant relationships, this step involves an experiential and philosophical exploration of what it means to be loyal.

Love questers will attempt to master three major facets of loyalty: loyalty to ourselves; loyalty to those we love and loyalty to all our espoused values.

Loyalty is such a well-worn word that it might appear we can take its meaning for granted. That would be a mistake. At this level of love intelligence there is nothing simple about the concept either in the rarefied machinations of our minds or in the feelings of our hearts. We can still be dismayed and profoundly hurt by disloyalty from someone we love. Conversely, we can still be overwhelmed with guilt and remorse if we betray someone we love or an honourable cause we believe in.

Betrayal is not always premeditated and is not necessarily caused by lust, hate, greed or jealousy. It can result from a lack of awareness, care, respect, steadfastness or courage. For instance, let's think about courage. There are many different forms of cowardice that can adversely affect loyalty. Common examples are: being party to some nasty ill-founded gossip about someone in our social circle; not passing on evidence of an affair to a close friend who is ignorant of their partner's infidelity; avoiding involvement in a violent or abusive relationship we witness because we don't like confrontation; failing to confess we've broken a shared couple commitment; telling someone we love what we think they want to hear rather than being truthful about our own thoughts and feelings and being disingenuous about behaviour we are ashamed of with individuals we love because we are afraid of their displeasure. There are many ways of being disloyal.

Historically, loyalty was highly prized because it enabled families, societies and nations to function with some certainty. It relied on a social pecking order and was underpinned by codes of honour which defined obligations and expectations. So, words like faithfulness, fidelity, homage, devotion, allegiance, obedience and constancy all imply loyalty. Rules about loyalty and definitions of loyal behaviour have been important milestones in human evolutionary development and this includes the institution of marriage.

Before we discuss a modern approach to loyalty, I want you to think about two love triangles from the past. The circumstances of their relationships are very different from our own, however the theme of love betrayed has ancient origins in human history and is therefore worthy of our attention. I want you to consider what the stories teach us about the nature of betrayal and what is the learning that can help us reconcile conflicting loves and loyalties on our own lives.

Firstly, I want to draw your attention to the ancient love story of King David and Bathsheba from Hebrew literature in the Old Testament [2 Samuel. 11:2–12:24]. King David was a highly evolved soul for his time in human history as demonstrated by his evocative Psalms recorded in the Old Testament and by his anointment as king when he was still a young man. He won the right to kingship by popular acclaim after King Saul and his son Jonathan were slain in battle. For those of you unfamiliar with David's story, you might like to explore his psychohistory further, including his famous slaying of the giant Goliath when he was just a boy. However, it's not David's great deeds but his fall from grace over his relationship with Bathsheba that's pertinent to our discussion. This is not to devalue the great love David and Bathsheba had for one another which produced David's heir to the throne, King Solomon. But even though he was a highly evolved soul, David was human and open to sin and error like any of us. His story is interesting because it recounts how David struggled with guilt when he violated the values of his own conscience.

The story goes like this. King David had several wives because polygamy was socially acceptable in his ancient culture. One day David was on his balcony when he spied a neighbour, Bathsheba, about to bathe. Bathsheba was naked and David was filled with lust for her. Lust is a normal human sexual drive so that wasn't a problem. It's what David chose to do with his lustful instincts that became the problem. For Bathsheba wasn't a slave, or prostitute and she wasn't single. Bathsheba was married to Uriah, a Hittite, serving in David's army. Accounts differ about what took place but it is generally accepted David ordered Uriah to the front line. Uriah was predictably, and conveniently, killed in battle. The marriage between David and Bathsheba then took place. Whether or not their first born was conceived before the marriage, the baby boy was sickly from birth and only lived a short while. David believed the death of his son was punishment for his *sin* and he underwent a period of penitence and fasting to make amends.

There are several ways of interpreting this story, especially as Bathsheba is one of the great matriarchs of Jewish history. I think for those of us looking back over time and making sense of love's evolutionary progress, we can reassure ourselves that psycho-spiritual growth has never been straight forward. We may not face the gender power imbalance implicit in David and Bathsheba's story, but many of us will recognise the agony and ecstasy of falling-in-love or lusting after someone inappropriately. Do we betray those we love to be true to our feelings, or do we betray our true feelings to keep the peace by saying and doing nothing? And what do we do when we break rules we believe in? As we are all capable of error and sin, I think the important message of this story is to address guilty feelings.

Guilt can be a useful tool if we are prepared to learn. Through the healing process of self-awareness, remorse, repentance and forgiveness we can make changes that neutralise our transgressions, although in some instances we may still be left with karmic debt that needs to be repaid in future incarnations. Understanding our own motives and seeking forgiveness is the key to removing feelings of guilt. Personally, I'm not sure how we can truly forgive ourselves without experiencing God's unconditional love and grace. But as you'll understand by now, this view of God's love is this author's philosophical bias.

Another fascinating story of love and betrayal is the legend of King Arthur, Queen Guinevere and Sir Lancelot du Lac, commonly referred to as Lancelot. The role of Lancelot in the Holy Grail saga is useful for our discussion of evolutionary psycho-spiritual development because he was unable to attain the Grail in his lifetime, even though he wanted to.

Lancelot was a hero knight in King Arthur's court. He reached the pinnacle of physical prowess and skill in arms and was renowned for his courtliness. However, his love and admiration for King Arthur's wife, Guinevere, went beyond the medieval code of chivalry and he had an adulterous affair with her. Here was a man juggling conflicting loyalties – a desire to be a perfect knight, an allegiance to his famous king, passionate love for Guinevere and a burning ambition to find the Holy Grail which could confer immortality on the successful quester.

Because of his transgression, Lancelot is allowed a glimpse of the Grail but is prevented from reaching it. Interestingly, Lancelot's son Galahad appears in the story as a perfect knight and becomes the leader of the three men who do achieve the Grail.

The love triangle of Arthur, Guinevere and Lancelot demonstrates the complexities of loyalty any of us might encounter in our searches for love and knowledge. After the great King Arthur dies, Guinevere enters a religious priory and becomes a nun, eventually rising to the rank of abbess. Lancelot returns from his Grail quest a broken figure in many ways. He settles in a hermitage and eventually becomes a priest. Although Lancelot lives his life in penitence and prayer, he never stops loving Guinevere and dies six weeks after her death. The haunting nature of Guinevere and Lancelot's love story not only highlights the power of love's passion but also alerts us to the idea that finding the perfect partner is not the end goal of love development. It can be a wonderful step on the way but it's not the answer to the final riddle of self-actualisation and becoming a master of love.

In both these examples from the past, we can see that love conflicts have an honoured place in human evolutionary development. If we fast forward to twenty-first century, we can agree that this is still the case. The social changes of the twentieth century may have altered the circumstances but not the underlying dilemmas of love and loyalty. Nowadays, no one living in a Western democracy is required to stay in an unhappy marriage. It may be a revolutionary thought right now but I'm sure the time will come when couples only stay together if both partners are happy and fulfilled and both believe in the integrity of their union.

Conditional commitments based on love and respect which are open to constant revision will become popular marriage paradigms. Parting will be relatively easy and there will be no social stigma attached to being divorced or single. When we remove obedience from the definition of loyalty and insert the word respect, we have a very different way of comprehending and practising the art of loyalty.

Common sources of loyalty conflict in Middle Adulthood can occur between the differing emotional needs of lovers, partners, parents and children. This can become much more complicated if we become involved in the process of remarriage and stepfamily formation. Outside our domestic situations, loyalty tests can occur with friends, colleagues, bosses and acquaintances in the social networks that make up our lives.

When we take a broad view, it becomes obvious that tests of loyalty help us sort out who we are, what we believe in and what goals are important to us going forward. So often in the past we projected labels of disloyalty onto the sinful or hurtful behaviour of others and ignored our own disloyal motivations. If we want to progress our understanding of love and promote ourselves to the next step on the Love Path, we need to wrestle with the concept of loyalty in personal and meaningful ways.

Most couples I met who attended counselling after an adulterous affair found the most difficult aspect of their situation to heal was the loss of trust and the ongoing hurt of disloyalty. Indeed, some would say it wasn't the sexual act itself that caused the most pain but the lies and feeling foolish because they had believed in the sanctity of their marriage.

This veil of illusion always causes great distress if it is removed.

For couples who recommit to monogamous marriage after an affair there is often an uncomfortable discovery that unhealed hurts, misunderstandings and perceived disrespect have been played out in their sexual relationship. It was through my work with couples who found happiness again after affairs that I witnessed the awesome healing power of love and forgiveness. I came to the conclusion that we are all prone to disloyalty at various times in our lives and until we clean up our own back yards we can't really comment on the disloyalty of others.

I believe the process of loyalty begins with respect. The more we respect ourselves, the more likely we are to choose a life of integrity: albeit integrity on our own terms and not definitions of integrity mandated by others. And the more we respect ourselves, the more we will want to be surrounded by people we respect as much as ourselves. As night follows day, respect engenders loyalty. This type of loyalty is not based on fear or rules, but on admiration and love. We freely offer our loyalty because we want to.

Linda Goodman suggests the eighth love initiation is ruled by the sun sign Scorpio and is characterised by the statement 'I desire'. She linked desire in this instance to sexual desire. Goodman says the lesson to be learnt is that love is surrender and the teaching for others is that love is passion.

My interpretation of the eighth love step is that although libidinous energy fuels human intimacy, if we want to maintain ongoing respect in partnerships and friendships, we need to be able to demonstrate loyalty. Loyalty deepens trust. It allows us more freedom to experience the psycho-spiritual connection between eroticism and romance in partnerships and between soul-connection and affection in family relationships and friendships. Individuals on the eight step of love maturity teach others that loyalty is honourable and cannot be bought on the cheap or traded for social approval.

Step Nine
Later Adulthood – Sacrifice
(Passion Versus Contentment)

Later Adulthood is the third and final step of the University Stage on the Love Path. This ninth step of love development requires us to amalgamate all our previous learnings and use this advanced level of psycho-spiritual functioning to help others. We can model our personal authority and confidence informally for anyone who is interested and use our expertise formally in a variety of professional roles.

Later Adulthood on the Love Path schema hypothetically refers to the age group from forty-four years to fifty-five years. For many of us, this will be the last step of love development in our current incarnation. We may feel we have struggled enough and now want to look forward to a comfortable life of contentment, filled with good friends, good times and bucket loads of adventurous fun. Or we may be one of the rare individuals who reached enlightenment in an earlier incarnation and will therefore have no need to repeat the tests of the next stage, Transfiguration.

For those who want to continue the ascent up the Pyramid of Wisdom, the challenge will be to forgo material contentment in favour of continuous passionate enquiry. This may not be as difficult as it sounds because we are likely to be hooked on the pleasure of learning. We may also become intrigued by the notion that it is theoretically possible to find the Grail and become masters of love within this lifetime. Indeed, we may have already been personally approached by Spirit and told that the goal is possible if we stay true to the quest.

Let's now return to the subject at hand, the tasks to be mastered on step nine of the Love Path. Whether we wish to maintain our psycho-spiritual maturity or whether we are preparing to advance to the next stage of development, the challenge we face is learning to accept there is a psychospiritual purpose attached to suffering.

Later Adulthood is generally associated with the physiological process of middle age. We are confronted, one way or another, with a set of circumstances which can be referred to as a mid-life crisis. This crisis may be mild or severe. But, like all crises, there is an impetus for change. Science in the future may mitigate many of the physical aspects of aging. However, we cannot change the accumulation of experience. We can choose to either stay stuck in a picture of ourselves that isn't evolving or accept the inevitability of aging. Staying stuck is likely to impede the growth of self-awareness as energy and resources get channelled toward external markers of success, such as youthful appearance, physical beauty, career achievements, wealth and popularity.

Wisdom doesn't give away her jewels easily. We shrivel our chances of attaining self-actualisation if we ignore or forget to listen to our intuitive Christos connection. In a modern world, it's very easy to become pre-occupied with superficial issues and taxing problems that sap our energy and try our patience. We can easily lose heart or become bored. It's then easy to turn to any of our favourite addictions or dependencies or search for a new love object to make ourselves feel better. But short-term fixes don't last. And if stresses mount, we become vulnerable to burnt out.

A mid-life crisis, provided it's not prolonged or totally over-whelming, can be useful. It wakes us out of our materialistic slumbers. It encourages us to go searching for answers to personal problems as well as life's mysteries in a more general sense. Occasionally, a mid-life crisis produces existential doubt, debilitating self-criticism and suicidal thoughts. In spite of all our earlier learning and progress we may need external help to get back on track. This is most likely to happen when we are faced with a number of losses occurring over a brief period of time or when we become socially isolated because of changed circumstance. Death of a child, spouse or parent, marital separation, redundancy and bankruptcy are obvious examples. Grief becomes complicated and a spiral of mental unwellness can quickly feel like we are sinking into a dark hole. Although full recovery may take some time, we can begin to feel better with some robust yet sensitive professional help.

By the ninth step of love development we've accumulated a lot of life experience. We've learnt it's important not to give up or give in, yet hope can still be challenged. Sometimes all that is asked of us is to accept situations of suffering outside our control. Self-love and self-respect can be strengthened when we recognise the growth of resilience. Even when we struggle with the seeming unfairness of certain situations, we need to retain a belief that this has nothing to do with deserving or underserving and everything to do with proving our true worth. This is the only way our human evolution can be spiritually authentic.

By step nine, many love questers want an independent conscious connection with Spirit. The pull of the material world is strong, so it helps if we feel that our relationship with Spirit doesn't require intermediaries or special places of worship. If we don't consciously pursue spiritual awareness, we may lose ground and ultimately lose what faith we have. It's okay to choose not to go higher up the Pyramid of Wisdom, or even back track a little. However it's sad to lose ground through neglect or a deliberate retreat down the path because we don't like what's being asked of us. Losing faith inevitably results in a vague sense of emptiness or more pronounced bitterness.

Faith is maintained in Later Adulthood by continuing a passionate interest in love in all its colours and manifestations. We have gained experience and expertise in matters of the heart and are adept at creating circles of intimacy that are physically and emotionally safe. Even if we are single, we are important sources of wisdom in the world and will frequently find ourselves mentoring children and adolescents, whether as parents, grandparents, teachers and coaches or in some other roles.

One of the developmental tasks we may encounter on this step of the Love Path is the sexual experience referred to as the Kundalini awakening. The spiritual purpose of this event is to separate our base and sacral chakras. While some highly evolved souls may meditate to induce this change at an earlier age, I think it's wise to let this process happen naturally. Late Adulthood is an ideal time because we have the background experience necessary to manage our sexual intelligence without hurting others unwittingly or unnecessarily.

For those of us who were raised with Judeo-Christian values, the experience of the Kundalini awakening can take us by surprise. We can help ourselves by becoming informed about the Hindu chakra system, though we don't need to become experts. Liz Simpson's explanation of how to use some knowledge of chakras to assist our own healing is a useful primer. And for students of psychology, I would recommend John E. Nelson's, *Healing the Split.* Nelson's theories of integrating Eastern philosophy and Western neuropsychiatry to assist clients suffering mental illness are based on his own experience with patients. In the book he references a case of the Kundalini experience causing mental distress.

If valued as a spiritual gift to be managed wisely, the Kundalini awakening marks the beginning of a process to broaden and deepen our understanding of unconditional love. If misused because of desires for temporal power and ego based sensual pleasure, the results can be catastrophic. When cult leaders, clerics, gurus and high priestesses hurt the innocent because of inflated egos, their victims are in danger of having their faith in a loving God damaged beyond repair in this lifetime. Furthermore, victims may become wary of professionals trying to help because their trust in authority figures has been shattered. There are clear warnings about misusing the Kundalini experience or any other spiritual gift that is bestowed on us. Unless we have some awareness of our errors and sins and are prepared to do something about it, our soul personalities are much better off remaining in ignorance. In the end, we all have to account for the way we've used our time on earth.

Later Adulthood requires us to sort the wheat [wisdom] from the chaff [foolishness]. We will encounter various tests to ensure our worthiness including the meaning of sacrifice. As mentioned previously, sacrifice has an evolutionary history and is concerned with invoking spiritual holiness. A personal sacrifice involves grieving and accepting the loss of someone or something we hold dear.

Growing Christ-consciousness is a personal journey. While differences in psycho-spiritual development can cause problems in intimate relationships at any age, they can become major hurdles during Later Adulthood. These issues can be resolved if partners are prepared to give each other freedom to follow the yearnings of their hearts while maintaining a commitment of fidelity. My advice for relationships in this phase of life is to experiment and laugh a lot. Foster some mystery, respect differences and assume nothing. Enjoy the process of creating romance by embracing some new interests together and by keeping passion alive through shared experiences and thoughtful attentiveness. We can handle differences when individual perceptions are honoured and when no partner feels less valued than the other. Some partners may choose to create a couple culture that doesn't follow the usual rules of togetherness or doesn't require fidelity for their love commitment to hold true. As long as any new arrangements feel fair and amicable, it doesn't matter what others think. There are no right or wrong ways, only ways that make us happy or unhappy.

For some of us sameness has never be the goal. We relish our differences. We jealously guard our right to individual thought, feelings and intuitions. The ingredients of long-term sexual passion are respect, admiration and fascination. If we want trust to be centre stage, the task is to create couple boundaries that are secure but sufficiently permeable to allow each partner opportunities to pursue personal growth.

Sometimes differences are too big to be resolved. We can recognise this when partners say that although they still love each other, they are no longer in love with one another. Therapy can be useful but doesn't guarantee both partners will want to stay in the relationship long-term. If a request for more freedom turns out to be the beginning of the end of the relationship, accept it with grace. Learning to let love go without bitterness or regret is an advanced love skill. We can experience the emotional pain of grief while continuing to explore new beginnings for ourselves.

Linda Goodman suggests the ninth love initiation is governed by the sun sign Sagittarius and is characterised by the statement 'I see'. She says the lesson to be learnt is that love is loyalty and the teaching for others is that love is honesty.

My interpretation of the ninth love step is that there are two major tasks to be accomplished. The first task is to relate the issue of loss to the spiritual value of sacrifice. The second is to integrate all the knowledge and skills we have accumulated during earlier steps of our development and use our knowledge altruistically. The teaching for others is that people who have acquired this level of hard-won wisdom are exemplary role models irrespective of their social backgrounds or current material circumstances.

Unless we've achieved enlightenment in a previous incarnation, completing step nine faces us with an option. We can remain in the contentment of having achieved a great deal or we can apply to go further. The biblical phrase, *many are called but few are chosen,* aptly describes the selection process we engage in if we wish to continue a passionate quest for personal psycho-spiritual evolution.

Stage Four
Transfiguration: (Compassion)

When we graduate to stage four on any path of the Pyramid of Wisdom it is a notable achievement. My interpretation of this advanced psycho-spiritual development is that we can now consider ourselves Grail heroes. We have earned the key that allows us re-entry into the symbolic Garden of Eden. Our overall task during the next three steps of development is to earn the other keys to heaven Jesus referred to in the New Testament. We achieve this goal by finding a route through the hedge of knowledge that surrounds the Tree of Life. The fruit from the Tree of Life, which is also represented in religious literature as the body and blood of Christ, gifts the successful querent immortality.

The trek through the hedge of knowledge is often likened to an adventure through a labyrinth. We are given clues at various junctures to assist our choices and understandings. As each route is unique and contains tests that are only relevant to our own self-growth, I am not supplying a maze guide for those choosing to follow the Love Path. Rather, I'm presenting some ideas to reflect on with the added intention of providing reassurance that the path at times can seem lonely and strange.

We live in interesting times. Neuroscience is uncovering fresh information every day. We now know that the neuronic patterns of brain development are so complex they reflect patterns of energy in the observable universe. This supports the ancient spiritual belief that it is below as it is above, and vice versa. For the lonely pilgrim ascending the final levels of psycho-spiritual development, there is much to ponder. The important skills are to maintain focus on the end goal; avoid wasting energy on dead end projects and arguments that can't be resolved; and trust destiny that we will be given the necessary help at the times we need it.

During the Transfiguration Stage of love development we are likely to witness situations involving psychic phenomena. We will also become more aware of our own inherent psychic abilities. This process will not be straight forward. The gate keepers of exoteric knowledge in Western societies generally look askance at any claims of paranormal experience outside mainstream religious institutions. And it's absolutely understandable that anyone, including partners, family members or friends, would also express their scepticism if they haven't had a personal psychic experience of their own. I urge patience. All that we need to do to help future researchers in this field by keeping accurate accounts of our experiences in a logbook or periodic journal. Hopefully, in time, common threads of experience will be identified across many personal narratives from many different cultures.

The developmental theme for the Transfiguration stage of the Love Path is compassion. Like all love concepts it has a spiral of meaning. We will discover new levels of understanding the deeper we go through a combination of experience and reflection.

The three steps that comprise this fourth stage of love development are experienced as a structured set of circumstances to grow our self-awareness. It's quite likely that we won't be able to make sense of all we discover until we've completed our climb. We will be confronted by situations that alert us to our own strengths and weaknesses, and to the complexity of life itself. As we progress through this experiential process of growing compassion, we will lose our socially constructed outer layer of niceness and sentimentality in favour of developing integrated congruency.

The process of Transfiguration will change us. This can be unsettling for partners, family members, friends and colleagues. We need to remember that Jesus talked about bringing a sword. The symbolic Grail or Christos sword cuts away deceit, false pride and plastic superficiality. It doesn't mean we stop having fun or that we cut the bonds of affection with those we love. On the contrary, where mutual respect and admiration thrive so too will our enjoyment of the companionship. Sometimes, though, the only way other people can deal with our growing confidence, is to try to undermine us or put us down. Consequently, it's common during the final ascent of the Pyramid of Wisdom to spend more time alone and to avoid negative situations.

As we journey up this final stage of love development, we begin to understand how important it is to stay true to ourselves. All we really need to do is to be gentle with ourselves and have clear boundaries in our relationships with others. The journey to self-actualisation is personal to us. We don't need to justify our choices or attitudes nor do we need to prove we're right. The best course of action is to choose our intimate circle wisely and spend time with individuals who appreciate and respect us.

The final comment I want to make about this stage of development, is that we gain much more than we lose. The shape of the pyramid we've been climbing means the four paths of development have been getting closer. Stage four is generally an interesting phase in our lives when we can make universal connections more easily. It also becomes quicker to traverse other paths and complete spirals of learning. And, in the process, we are likely to meet other individuals who share common understandings with us even though their backgrounds and life experiences may have been very different.

Attaining Christhood is different for each of us and there is no template of perfection. Each of us retains our essential soul personality. We can therefore celebrate our differences, unique styles, quirky mannerisms, special traits and abilities. The character flaws that require attention along the way are generally those aspects of ourselves we haven't been aware of or wanted to acknowledge because the picture we have of ourselves is skewed or inflated. For example, each of us is important in the scheme of things but no one is more important in spiritual terms. Unless we learn to love others as ourselves and develop unwavering integrity, we won't achieve Christhood. For the problem with unexamined character traits and unhealed emotional wounds is that we remain vulnerable to sin or error. The final stages of psychospiritual development are a bit like participating in a spiritual SAS training camp.

As more and more individuals reach the Pyramid of Wisdom summit and are prepared to publicly record their experience because it becomes safer to do so, we will begin to accumulate evidence of psycho-spiritual transformation occurring in many places and different cultures. From the many we will be able to extrapolate a typical transformative process. This will assist those working in clinical practice when they are working with clients who are struggling to give meaning to their experience, especially when it appears to be extreme or bizarre.

The requirement in the final stages of psycho-spiritual evolution to be independent and self-focused can be mistakenly labelled as narcissistic. That's why it's important for questers of psycho-spiritual knowledge to be careful who they consult professionally. As psycho-spiritual progress is often accompanied by periods of uncertainty and grief, an individual's behaviour may seem like pathology rather than a normal reaction to extraordinary events. Best for Grail heroes to find counsellors who can listen without presumptuous judgements' and who are prepared to offer psychological holding while stability is needed.

Step Ten
Mature Adulthood – Freedom (Fortitude Versus Capitulation)

Mature Adulthood is the tenth step of the Love Path. It may follow the chronological guide of fifty-five to sixty years of age or may occur much earlier in the lives of highly evolved soul personalities. Whatever our age, the change process of Transfiguration which begins with a sacrifice will not be completed until step twelve when we will undergo the experience of spiritual rebirth.

Although our body is not going to die, we cannot experience spiritual rebirth without some part of our persona or current personality dying or perhaps being killed off is another way of viewing it. The Tarot card, The Hanged Man, contains the ultimate mystical representation of this process. Although the card is used for divination purposes to represent any sacrifice that allows the querent to see life more clearly, within its symbolism we find the clue that has always been there for those on the final part of the journey to reach the Grail. For although the Fool is suspended upside down, dangling by a thread around one ankle, he already is wearing the golden disc or halo of the sun-god.

For those looking for ancient references to this transformative process, the *Book of Job* in the Old Testament of the *Holy Bible* is a useful reference. The story tells of a very rich man who was not only a very good man but also one who worshipped the Lord. Satan approaches God with the proposition that the only reason Job is devout is because God is blessing him. God agrees to let Satan to take away Job's wealth, his children and finally his health to see whether Job remains faithful to God.

The experiment proceeds and Job undergoes terrible suffering. Three well-meaning friends don't understand what is taking place and insist Job must be doing something wrong for God to be punishing him like this. Despite the criticism Job stays faithful to God. After the appearance of another bystander, named Elihu, who criticises both sides of the argument, Job is left alone, still declaring his innocence and asking God for explanations. God does finally appear to Job but instead of offering him an explanation for his suffering, rebukes him for talking too much. Nevertheless, because Job has withstood the test and remained faithful, God blesses him. Job is made twice as wealthy as he was before.

The story has many layers which become more apparent if our own situation seems to mirror any or all of Job's trials. Whether or not our testing echoes Job's trials, we are in a much better situation because evolutionary progress has allowed us access to information to resolve our dilemmas and caring support to help heal our grief. And we understand the purpose of our testing. It's this awareness that we are living for a cause that has become greater than ourselves that allows us to master this step with open loving hearts.

Our task is to stay resilient, process the feelings that arise and maintain a direct conversation with Spirit that is increasingly mature. Like Job we can remain faithful to our truth, however unlike Job we can continue to search for answers instead of expecting God to hand over wisdom before we are psycho-spiritually ready to receive it. Most importantly, we don't need to hang onto bitterness the way Job did. Bitterness is the natural outcome of disillusionment, ignorance, and an unexamined sense of entitlement.

For students of psychology, I recommend Edinger's analysis of the Job story which he describes as an encounter with the Self. Edinger makes the important connection that the description of Satan in the *Book of Job* approximates the feminine personification, Wisdom in *Ecclesiasticus* [Edinger, p. 93. Jerusalem Bible 4:11–21]. In the passage from *Ecclesiasticus*, we are told that Wisdom nurtures her followers and cares for all who seek her. Then we are given a description of the way she disciplines those she loves. She tests her heroes through winding ways. When she believes she can trust them, she will lead them back to the straight road and reveal her secrets to them. What is interesting for our discussion is that Wisdom has many names including Sophia, Goddess of the Grail, the Black Virgin and Goddess of Love. It is therefore a recognition of our status as Grail or love heroes that our knowledge and intentions are tested to prove our worthiness and steadfastness.

The sacrifice that propelled our graduation from step nine begins an intense period of testing. We need to demonstrate that we have fortitude, that we will not capitulate under attack, pressure or criticism. Remaining loyal to our own truth may cost us social approval and popularity, even friends, careers and family relationships. It's useful to remember that like Job, these losses are not necessarily permanent. We will be given opportunities to work with fortitude for long-term redemption. The old saying, first they love you, then they hate you, then they love you again is a precis of the process we are likely to endure. However, by the time we are in favour again, it's likely popularity won't mean what it once did.

The purpose underlying a conscious sacrifice for love is to know oneself better and therefore, ultimately, to know God. This interpretation fits well with the story of little Colton Burpo who maintains he visited heaven during a near death experience in hospital just before his fourth birthday. His pastor father, Todd Burpo, later recorded the amazing insights this young boy offered over following months. Colton said that he met Jesus in heaven who told him the reason he died on the cross was so that those on earth *'could come see my dad'*.

Come see my dad gives us a completely different picture of the purposeful sacrifice Jesus made. Looking back, we can hypothesise that the bulk of populace living at the time of the crucifixion were insufficiently evolved to recognise the spiritual purpose of conscious sacrifice. The idea that Jesus died to save us from our own sins was an intermediary step in human psycho-spiritual evolution. We can now link the phrase, *come see my dad,* with the ancient gnostic belief that we come to know God through knowing ourselves and with modern psychological theory that self-awareness supports the growth of emotional intelligence and moral acuity.

The testing on step ten reminds us of the directive Jesus left for his followers, to pick up our own cross and follow his example to Christhood. The theories of Carl G. Jung can help us interpret this ancient teaching. Jung is famous for his study of mythology and universal archetypes, and he believed the cross and the numeral 4, have always symbolised mana or life power. Edward F. Edinger has proposed that the meaning of picking up one's cross is that we accept and consciously realise the unique pattern of our own wholeness. I would add that a pattern of psycho-spiritual wholeness can also be termed Christhood. So, for those wishing to achieve the immortality of Christhood, there is a need to master some testing which equates to picking up one's own cross.

Linda Goodman suggests that the tenth love initiation is governed by the sun sign, Capricorn, and is characterised by the statement 'I use'. She says the lesson to be learnt is that love is unselfishness and that the teaching for others is that love is wisdom. Goodman also postulated that the theme for this stage of love development is experience.

My interpretation of the tenth step of love development is that the change process known as the crucifixion of the persona or false ego has begun. Like Goodman I believe that experience is the teacher here and this step can't be negotiated by an intellectual exercise of comprehension alone. The love hero is learning to be authentically themselves as they deal to negative traits and errors of thought and behaviour within themselves. Psychological literature refers to the dark side of our personality as our shadow which is a useful way to conceptualise it. If we only know our good and light side, we remain ignorant of life's deepest mysteries. I believe the skill to be learnt on the tenth step of the Love Path is fortitude as the individual is tested many times to prove their worthiness. The teaching for others is respect for mysteries beyond current understanding.

Step Eleven
Senior Adulthood – Generosity (Humility Versus Pride)

Senior Adulthood is the penultimate step on the Love Path and approximates the years from sixty to sixty-five on the guideline provided. Having mastered the tests and rigours of step ten, step eleven is a comparative breeze. All we need to do is consciously expand our self-awareness and generously share our knowledge of love with all who are interested to learn more.

It doesn't matter whether we are in a committed partnership, single and dating, or single and not dating, other people will be drawn to our positivity, warmth and life experience. I liken this step to the peripatetic teacher who has a following wherever he or she goes. We probably won't have a following like Jesus did when he was preaching from mountain sides or lake shores to soul hungry crowds. But we will meet strangers in unexpected ways and in unexpected places who want to engage us in conversations which rapidly become deep and meaningful. This will feel like synchro-destiny in action.

Step eleven can be described as a joyful experience even when circumstances are difficult. This is because Spirit includes us a lot more in the meaning underpinning our particular human experience. We can appreciate the coincidences, jokes and wild psychic events put on for our personal benefit. Even though we may receive channelled psychic messages identifying areas of self-growth still needing attention, we are likely to feel privileged and awed by the attention we receive.

We are now ready for some very fine tuning, or in the analogy of wood carving, very fine sanding. Common stumbling blocks to progress at this advanced level of love development are stubbornness and false pride. Given all we've endured previously, these challenges can come as bolts out of the blue. After all, it was partly our stubbornness that ensured we didn't capitulate when the going got tough. Now we discover we need to temper this character trait and listen more closely to our own intuition. And then there is the topic of false pride. That requires some deep self-reflection not only to understand what Spirit is asking of us but learning how to recognise the difference between true pride which leads to humility and false pride which can lead to us thinking we know best and therefore behaving with a lack of sensitivity. Although step eleven is wondrous in many ways, we won't progress to the next step until all the work is done.

To help us focus on the tasks of step eleven, my suggestion is to explore mythology and religious tests and icons for personal clues of understanding. One topic that is very useful to research at a deeper level is forgiveness. The traditional Lord's Prayer can help us particularly if we re-word the text to comply with gender equality. The prayer then becomes *Our Lord and Lady's Prayer*. The prayer teaches us that not only are we required to learn how to forgive those who trespass [verb] against us, we need to ask Spirit in a meaningful way that our own trespasses [noun] be forgiven. When we look up the archaic meaning of trespass, both noun and verb, we can interpret what is being asked of us: forgive us our sins or errors that are offensive as we will forgive those who do wrong or commit offences against us. In other words, while we are asking for divine forgiveness for our sins and misdemeanours, which at this level of psycho-spiritual comprehension will be pretty clear to us, we also asking for the maturity and insight to forgive others who intentionally want to hurt us in some way. We are stating we want to reach an evolutionary level of development that allows us to follow the maxim of Jesus Christ to love our enemies.

It can be a surprise for followers on the Love Path that some people will feel so negatively about us that they can be described in spiritual terms as our enemies. This can be particularly hurtful if we previously considered some of these people as our friends whom we cared about deeply. An evolved way of handling this is to continue loving people who hurt us [i.e. forgive them for they know not what they do], and then distance ourselves both physically and emotionally so we don't stay on a merry-go-round of conflicted feelings. Conflicted feelings are energy-draining and time wasting. A period of healing grief allows us to let go old attachments and ready ourselves for the work ahead.

I don't think we can ascend the Transfiguration stage of love development without some enemies entering our personal dramas. Some people just won't care for us and they may then be compelled to make attacks on our morals, appearances, motivations and personalities either in public or insidiously through gossip. Unfair or erroneous judgements from strangers can fleetingly hurt. But much harder to bear, and to heal from, are the emotional and psychic wounds inflicted on us by people whom we have loved very much. These wounds have the power to make us physically and emotionally sick. When we experience the destructive power of malicious gossip, we become more careful about not engaging in it ourselves.

Generosity at this level of psycho-spiritual functioning is a grand inclusive concept. Previously it's been relatively easy to be generous to partners, friends and family who show us kindness or to be generous towards strangers who are in obvious need when we have plenty. It's now much more of a challenge to be kind in our actions and generous in our spirit with enemies who are close at hand and who have emotionally hurt us. This is when love teaches us to be strong, yet humble. We will be given evidence that we are still loved and supported by Spirit. However, we will be guided to show kindness in our relationships with others even when our loving intentions are not reciprocated.

Mastering generosity on step eleven requires more of us than demonstrations of material kindness. I think it's what Jesus meant when he advised us to turn the other cheek. Pride is being dealt to. We need to let go the need for our individuality to be accepted or our subject reality to be understood. And, importantly, we need to accept that our enemies and adversaries are loved by Spirit, just like we are.

The crucifixion process deals to our persona or false ego. There is a shattering of our socially constructed persona so that it can be integrated with our true ego. Hubris is finally being dealt to. With an expanded view of generosity, we can pray for our enemies as well as our friends. And significantly, we lose the need to be important in the material world. This is the ultimate challenge. To see ourselves, and our friends, and our enemies as all part of the same humanity loved dearly by our mother/father god. It may serve love's purpose for us to experience a period of material or social dispossession to prove our worthiness and the purity of our intentions.

Let's return to the Parable of the Good Samaritan we discussed on step three. We can now interpret the parable more deeply as we recognise that generosity requires us to be as kind to ourselves as we are to others. This includes accepting all the parts of ourselves including our shadow aspects. John A. Sanford argues that the despised Samaritan, the stranger from another culture, represents the part of ourselves we have looked down on or ignored for so long. It is our kind internal voice of mercy which has the capacity to assist our healing to full psycho-spiritual health.

Linda Goodman suggests the eleventh love initiation is governed by the sun sign Aquarius and is characterised by the statement 'I know'. She says the lesson to be learnt is that love is Oneness and the teaching for others is that love is tolerance. Goodman also postulated this stage is dominated by the theme of idealism.

My interpretation of the eleventh step on the Love Path is similar in many ways to the ideas put forward by Goodman. Although this step is part of the crucifixion of the persona process that eventually results in Transfiguration, it's a step of dynamic action that is fuelled by idealism. Learning to be generous in our love requires focus and increased self-awareness. If we stay true to our mission and don't get side-tracked by a late challenge of ego-inflation, our pride gets dealt to and we naturally take on the humility of a servant of love. The tarot card, The Hermit, epitomises our development during Senior Adulthood. The Hermit teaches us not to be afraid of aloneness but to use our advanced understanding as a lantern of light for others following in our footsteps. The teaching for others is that true generosity comes from the heart without strings or conditions.

Step Twelve
Old Age – Integration
(Individuation Versus Attachment)

We have arrived at the final step on the Love Path. When we have completed the developmental love tasks of Old Age, we will ascend to the summit of the Pyramid of Wisdom and be ready for a splendid celebration of some sort. We can enjoy the accolades we receive from Spirit because we know we've truly earned them.

I have suggested that the hypothetical age bracket for Old Age is from sixty-five years to seventy years. If we reach this advanced standard of love functioning much younger, both in our understandings and in our skill set, others will naturally describe us as having the wisdom of an old soul.

The change process which began on step ten is completed on this step. The cleaning and pruning of our soul personality is complete and we are now ready to be transformed. We do this through a chrysalis-like experience from which we emerge fully integrated and enlightened. Spirit will find a way to confirm for us that we have reached the summit of the Pyramid of Wisdom and that our symbolic white robes have been swapped for psychic mantles of gold to signify our birth into Christhood. The alchemical process of turning lead to gold represents the journey of Transfiguration. We've had the impurities of sin removed so that we can shine in our own Christ-conscious light. At last we can be likened to little children because we have developed mature innocence with honest and loving intentions.

One of my clinical supervisors once described the choice of pursuing Transfiguration rather well. He suggested that many people are happy to remain like schooners sailing around the Pacific Ocean doing good at every port despite barnacles on their hulls and their interiors needing a refit. Then there are some who will not be content until they've refashioned themselves to win the race. This smaller group of individuals willingly undergo tests and trials to be the lightest, sleekest and technologically advanced sailing yachts on the planet so that they can win the race of their lives.

Those of us who chose to complete the last three steps on the Love Path are like racing yachts obsessed with winning the ultimate prize. It's interesting that the America's Cup for yachting greatness is an old ornate highly valuable trophy in the style that many of us envisage the Holy Grail chalice to be.

Integration, like tasks on earlier steps, requires time and understanding. We are excited by the changes we are making. However, we will also experience sadness as we let go the old and familiar parts of ourselves and aspects of our lifestyles that no longer serve our new identity and destiny. If we have been fortunate and have received information from Spirit about some of our past life personas and relevant karmic debt payments or repayments, we will find detaching from the delights of this world much easier. I therefore recommend past life regression for anyone at this level of development needing to fill in some gaps in their existential psychohistory.

We know love is eternal. There will always be special places in our hearts for loved ones no matter what we do in the future or where our destiny takes us. However, we are finally developing an independence that is free of obligations and any form of karmic debt going forward. We can appeal to Archangel Michael to sever psychic chords of attachment that are no longer needed or desired.

The old wise man described by Leo Tolstoy in *War and Peace* gives us an example of what to expect. He was said to love everyone but to have no lovers, to be friendly to everyone but to have no friends. While I don't believe we need to eliminate lovers, partners and friends from our lives in any literal sense, I think the underlying notion is correct. We will choose to retain close emotional bonds with loved ones, but we will not feel compelled to belong to any family, social group or human institution. Nor will we choose to remain in any personal relationship if it doesn't feel right for us.

When compassion becomes universal within us, we can love on a subliminal level that is pure and divine at its source and we no longer experience traditional boundaries of gender, sexual orientation, colour, culture, education, social class or religion. This doesn't make us soft touches for others to abuse, nor does it deny us the individual right to express our political and social views with forthrightness. It does, however, mean we are comfortable living life on our own terms without seeking anyone's approval.

While we remain on earth, we still function as humans. Our unique soul personalities may be preparing for different futures, yet we will still be immersed in the social and political issues of the day. We may believe in the rightness of a just war or we may adopt the stance of a pacifist. We may actively be involved in problematic or even controversial social issues or socially retreat and live like a hermit preferring to leave the act of arguing to others. There are no right or wrong ways of Mastering Old Age other than being true to our higher selves.

As we make progress on the twelfth step, we recognise that we've become like the parental figure in the parable of the prodigal son. At an earlier level of development, we discussed this parable as representing the importance of finding the rebel in ourselves so that we could experience life. Now we are ready to identify with the father in the story who instantly forgives his son and showers him with unconditional love. Coming home to ourselves has new meaning. We can bless the rebel and other shadow aspects of ourselves for all the learning they've helped us achieve. We are learning to be truly compassionate with ourselves so that we can be passionate to others in the same way without judgement or negative stereotyping.

When we graduate from step twelve, we can rightly call ourselves masters of love. We will use our remaining time on earth wisely and willingly share our hard-won wisdom with anyone who approaches us with respect and sensible questions.

Linda Goodman suggests the twelfth love initiation is governed by the sun sign Pisces and is characterised by the statement 'I believe'. She says the lesson to be learnt is that is that love is ALL and the teaching for others is that love is compassion. Interestingly, Goodman postulates that the theme for this final love development is submission.

My interpretation of this twelfth and final step on the Love Path is a little different. I consider integration rather than submission to be the vital task. This idea is not new. Carl G. Jung and others have postulated that an integration is vital to complete the individuation process that completes our true personality formation. In the process of achieving this level of self-actualisation the love hero begins a detachment from the material world without losing the ability for compassionate love. We are in the world but no longer of the world. This is no small feat. Fortunately, Spirit is with us all the way. And, of course, the physical process of aging assists a sense of detachment. We have discovered how to be at peace with ourselves.

The teaching for others is that an enlightened individual is no longer controlled by the usual societal and relational rules. The Osho Zen Tarot card, The Rebel, summarises this stage of development succinctly. We take responsibility for who we are and how we live our own truth. And becoming masters of love makes it is easy to believe that Love is All.

Select Bibliography

American Bible Society. *Holy Bible – Contemporary English Version*, NY, 1995
Astell, Christine. *Discovering Angels,* London, Duncan Baird, 2005
Barber Richard. *The Holy Grail: The History of a Legend*, London, Penguin, 2005
Burpo, Todd with Vincent, Lynn. *Heaven is for Real*, Nashville, Thomas Nelson, 2010
Campbell, Joseph with Moyers Bill. *The Power of Myth*, NY, Anchor Books, 1991
Chopra, Deepak. *Synchro Destiny*, London, Rider, 2004
Clydesdale, Ruth. *Secret Wisdom*, London, Arcturus, 2009
Cooper, Diana. *Angel Inspiration: How to change your world with angels*, London, Hodder & Stoughton, 2001
Cotterell, Arthur. *The Encyclopedia of Mythology*, London, Lorenz Books, 1996
Douglas, David. *The Atlas of Lost cults and Mystery Religions*, London, Godsfield Press, 2009
Edinger, Edward F. *Ego and Archetype*, Boston, Shambhala, 1972
El-Desouky, Ayman A. *Kahlil Gibran: An Illustrated Anthology*, London, Octopus, 2010
Faber, Lee. *Book of Angels*, London, Arcturus Publishing, 2010
Fromm, Erich. *The Art of Loving*, London, Unwin books, 1974
Gardiner, Philip with Osborn, Gary. *The Serpent Grail*, London, Watkins, 2005
Gibran, Kahlil. *The Prophet*, London, Pan Books, 1980
Goodman, Linda. *Linda Goodman's Love Signs*, London, Pan/Macmillan, 1980
Hamilton, Claire. *The Holy Grail: A Beginner's Guide*, London, Hodder & Stoughton, 2000
Harari, Yuval Noah. *Sapiens: A brief History of Humankind*, London, Vintage Books, 2011
Harold, Edmund. *Master Your Vibrations*, NSW, Grail, 2004
Harpur, Tom. *The Pagan Christ*, NSW, Allen & Unwin, 2005
Hart, Roger and Reed, A W. Maori Legends, Wellington, AH & AW Reed, 1972
Henry, Lewis C Edit. Five Thousand Quotations for all occasions, New York, Doubleday & Company Inc, 1945
Hind, Rebecca. *Sacred Places*, London, Carlton Books, 2007
Kalsched, Donald. *Trauma and the Soul: A psycho-spiritual approach to human development and its interruption*, East Sussex, Routledge, 2013
Matthews, Caitlin. *Sophia: Goddess of Wisdom, Bride of God*, Illinois, Quest Books, 2001

Monte, Christopher F. *Beneath the Mask: An Introduction to Theories of Personality [2nd Ed]*, NY, Holt, Rinehart and Winston, 1980

Nelson, John E. *Healing the Split: Integrating Spirit into Our Understanding of the Mentally Ill*, NY, State University of New York Press, 1994

O'Connell, Mark & Airey, Raje. *The Illustrated Encyclopedia of Signs and symbols*, London, Lorenz Books, 2007

Osho International Foundation, *Osho Zen Tarot*, London, Newleaf, 1996

Paterson, Helena. *The Celtic Tarot*, London, Thorsons, 1990

Ridge, Mian [Ed.]. *Jesus; The Unauthorised Version,* London, Profile Books, 2006

Ryan, Regina Sara. *Only God: A Bibliography of Yogi Ramsuratkumar,* Prescott Arizona, Hohm Press, 2004

Sandford, John A. *The Kingdom Within*, HarperSanFrancisco, 1987

Simpson, Liz. *The Book of Chakra Healing,* UK, Gaia Books, 2005

Spong, John Selby. *A New Christianity for a New World*, HarperSanFrancisco, 2001

Tarnas, Richard. *The Passion of the Western Mind*, London, Pimlico, 2010

The Delai Lama, *A Flash of Lightning in the Dark of Night: A Guide to the Bodhisattva's Way of Life,* Boston, Shambhala, 1994

The Holy Bible – King James Version, Oxford, University Press, 1940

Virtue, Doreen. *Archangels and Ascended Masters*, California, Hay House, 2003

Walsch, Neale Donald. *Conversations with God: an uncommon dialogue, Book 1*, Sydney, Hodder Headline, 1996

Webster, Richard. *Spirit Guides & Angel Guardians*, Minnesota, Llewellyn, 1998

Willis, Jim. *The Religion Book,* Detroit, Invisible Ink Press, 2004

Yogananda, Paramahansa. *Autobiography of a Yogi, 13th Ed,* California, Self-Realisation Fellowship, 1998